Why We Care

Choosing the Right Home Care Agency

Elizabeth,

Thank you so much for sending me a copy of your book. I am so proud of you for taking the leap of faith! This is a Kingdom Victory! Here's my book. I hope to speak with you soon. I'm speaking several times this year in MD, let's get together! Love always,

Steve "The Hurricane"

The Institute for Dignity and Grace
200 Craig Road Suite 203
Manalapan, NJ 07726

848 863-6603

http://dignityandgrace.info

Printed in the United States of America
Why We Care: Choosing the Right Home Care Agency

Print: ISBN 978-0-9979654-4-5

eBook: ISBN 978-0-9979654-3-8

Library of Congress Control Number: 2017957376

All proceeds from the sale of this book will be donated to The Institute for Dignity and Grace

Dedicated to seniors and the agency
owners who care for them

Table of Contents

Introduction

Every day, countless seniors fall and are seriously injured. Or they suffer heart attacks or strokes. Or they experience some kind of major medical episode. Any one of these events could have taken their lives, but instead leaves them impaired, their physical and/or mental abilities diminished. One day they were walking, driving, paying their bills, able to live and function independently. And then the next day, they are significantly or even completely dependent on another person for their care. The care choices now become a nursing home, assisted living or home health care.

This book was written so that we could tell the story about home health care for people who need it and the families who must make that decision. The story is told both through the experiences of home care providers and through the experiences of the real people who were able to find the help they needed when they needed it.

Why do we feel the need to tell this story? Because all too often, when a loved one goes from living an independent life to needing total care and assistance, there is no warning. There's no notice of what's to come and suddenly, you have to make very serious decisions in a short amount of time because typically, your loved one is coming home and there's nothing in place for their new needs.

What often comes next is a tremendous amount of pain and suffering, anxiety, fear of the unknown, and depression. Your loved one may be asking, "Why am I still alive? Why is this happening to me?" As a family member, you may be thinking, "I need help. I need a solution. I need to know that there are caring people out there who can help me in my situation."

Rest assured, for both patient and family, there is a solution. There is an answer to your questions and prayers, and it is in this book. In the following pages, you'll meet people who care, people who know how to provide one-on-one care, agency owners who have been doing this work for years—nurses, social workers, and other healthcare professionals who are truly in this for the right reasons. We are here for you.

To the children of the patients who now need care, those children who are in their 50s and 60s themselves, who have children of their own, maybe even grandchildren, who are still working a full-time job, this book is for you. You may have already turned to the almighty Google for answers. And there's so much information out there that you became overwhelmed. You're not sure how to decipher it, or where to go, or who to call. Everything is advertising, saying, "Call here." or "Do this." And you're searching for an answer. You're searching for a solution, not knowing that you might be pointed in the wrong direction. This book will help point you in the right direction.

You're going to find a collection of stories in these pages. Stories from entrepreneurs who founded home care agencies, as well as stories of the patients they have cared for over the years. You will learn the state those patients were in when their agency first came to them. What was the solution? How did they coordinate the care? What was the outcome?

You will find that you can relate to many of the patients' situations in the case studies we share with you. You yourself might be in the exact situation or one that's similar, and you may be able to find peace and comfort knowing that a positive outcome is possible. Even if the outcome is that your loved one passes away in the comfort of their home, where they were able to maintain their autonomy, as well as their dignity and grace in their final days. That's the purpose of this book.

We've realized that there really isn't anything available to the public providing the type of structure we offer in this book. These are actual situations, real case studies of patients and family members from across the country who found themselves in one of these predicaments where they said, "I need help and I need it now. And I'm not sure what the future holds."

Through the collected experiences of our contributors who provide these services, the reader will understand what is involved in home care, how much it costs, and what levels of care exist. Many people aren't even aware of the type of and extent of professional help that is available, or even that they might need it.

If a pipe breaks in your house, you probably call a plumber because you likely don't know much about plumbing. And since you don't know much about plumbing, you have to trust that the plumber knows what he's doing. But if you don't call the plumber, and try to fix it yourself with your limited or non-existent knowledge, you might end up with tremendous costs, annoyance, and extra time spent because eventually, you have to bring in the real professionals anyway. In the end, the whole ordeal could cost you double in what it could have if you'd just brought in a professional at the outset.

In this example with your house, you could say it's pain and suffering, but it's mostly financial and of course, frustration. When a family member needs special care, if you make the wrong decision from a healthcare standpoint, it could mean life or death. It could mean unnecessary hospitalizations, and unnecessary pain and suffering. And I have seen it happen. I've seen patients for whom home care was recommended, but it's a service, and it's not a free service. You have to pay for it. Some people are willing to forgo the services because they don't want to spend the money. And they end up going back into the hospital six months later, and their condition is ten times worse. It was preventable, though, if they had gotten professional care.

You don't want that to happen to your loved one. And it doesn't have to. There are good people out there, like our contributors, who can help you prevent unnecessary pain and suffering. That's the message in this book. Take action. Get it done right the first time. Avoid the unnecessary pain and suffering.

We are so passionate because we don't want anybody to suffer more than they have to. There are circumstances that you can't control. You can't control what disease someone gets, or dementia, or a serious fall. But once someone goes from being independent to dependent on someone else, you *can* control how you handle that situation. You can put measures in place like a home care provider to come into the home and help out on a daily basis for a just few hours, or all waking hours, or even 24/7. Your loved one can remain in the comfort of their home, as long as somebody has the financial means. But I'm not talking about millions of dollars.

Here's some perspective. Say a person receives home care four hours a day, seven days a week. This person has a terminal diagnosis. Maybe they had a stroke or a heart attack. They were in the hospital and now they're going home for the last six months of their life. This daily care includes pretty much all the needed help with the most important activities of daily living: making sure they take their meds, making sure they eat properly, making sure they exercise properly, making sure they have a shower and are dressed and ready for the day. Based on average national rates, the cost of what I just described is probably around $10,000 to $12,000 for six months. That is not an astronomical figure. That is affordable to most people, especially at the end of life. If they own their house, if they have retirement savings or other funds, $12,000, at the end of life, for their last six months is manageable. And they can't take that money with them.

Many times we see people, usually the patients, get caught up in inheritance. They want to leave a legacy to their children. They are resistant to the services, reluctant to spend their kids' inheritance on their own home care. The adult children, in my experience, don't care about the inheritance. They want the peace of mind that someone is there with their mother or father to care for them. So, make the decision to get the care, give the quality of life, and it will make it easier on your loved ones.

What I would suggest to you, as an adult child, go and see Mom. Spend time with her. Talk to Dad. Spend quality time making memories with him, so that when he passes away, or when Mom passes away, you have made memories that will last a lifetime. You'll know that you had closure, instead of having the common, "Do for Mom" because you have to give her a bath, and dress her, and make sure she's taking her meds, and everything else. All this on top of living your life and helping your children and grandchildren and work and everything else that you have to do, which can become next to impossible. When you have the care they need covered, you are able to come to visit, spend quality time, and make those memories while their time is drawing near.

That's why I'm so passionate about this, because all too often people say, "I wish I had more time. I wish I had more time." This book is going to enable you to see the stories of people who chose to get the care and because of that, they did have more time in the end. Their outcomes are positive. Families were able to come in and make those memories and have that closure before it was too late.

We want you to be inspired and confident as you read this book. We want you to believe that there are positive outcomes in very dark situations. Because you might be in a place of darkness right now, where there's this cloud, there's this frustration. There might even be anger and challenge everywhere you turn. You may be thinking, "I don't know what to do." This book will inspire you by shining light in your time of darkness, so you can find a way to a positive solution.

Steve "The Hurricane"™ Weiss

How to Use This Book

Use this book as a guide to help you find comfort in whatever situation you are in with your own loved one. Whether it's dementia, an unnecessary hospitalization, if you have two parents and one is declining while the other is healthy, or both parents are declining, or it's your spouse who needs help, there's someone who has been there before. Read through the entire book to get a general sense of each of our contributors. It will help you better understand the people who own these businesses from all across the country, and why they chose this line of business. Read all the interviews to become familiar with the diverse types of situations that exist out there.

Read through the table of contents and find a case study that best matches your own situation, and start there. Read those case studies that fit your situation the most closely, so that you can then better determine what to do for your loved one, based on "This is what happened to these individuals who are in a very similar situation to the one that I'm in. Here's what they did. I would like to proceed forward to have the same outcome as those individuals."

Use this book as a crystal ball into the future. "I'm in this situation now. I want to have a positive outcome. Let's see what other people who were in my situation did. How did they achieve their positive outcome? How can I proceed confidently, moving forward?" That's how you use this book.

The Institute for Dignity and Grace

The Institute for Dignity and Grace is a non-profit that was co-founded by Steve Weiss and Nicole Peretti, to act as an advocate for our senior population. We created it because we want to help prevent unnecessary hospitalizations and the needless pain and suffering for our seniors. The mission of the Institute is delivered in three parts.

The first part is to help coordinate care for patients suffering from five or more chronic conditions—as an example, heart disease, dementia, high blood pressure, COPD, and diabetes—while they're in the hospital or in a rehab within our health care system. Social workers and discharge planners at hospitals and rehab centers are often overworked and overburdened. They're carrying caseloads larger than they should, and they aren't fully aware or able to coordinate the free services or benefits that someone is entitled to receive. When hospital or rehab staff sees a patient suffering from five or more chronic conditions, they can contact The Institute. We'll then send the caseworker out at no charge to coordinate care for the individual and find what, if any, benefits they are entitled to receive.

The second part of the mission is for patients who need care but do not qualify for financial assistance. This could mean they are not a veteran and therefore aren't eligible for VA benefits, or if they are a veteran, their income exceeds the maximum for VA Aid and Attendance benefits. It could also mean they don't qualify for the Medicaid benefit, based on their income and assets. In these cases, The Institute will provide care for up to four hours a day, seven days a week, for the first 30 days after a hospitalization.

Why does The Institute offer this? Because it has been proven that when someone has daily help with custodial care after a hospitalization, meaning those activities of daily living such a bathing, toileting, transferring, getting dressed, meal preparation and so on, the likelihood of a readmission is greatly reduced.

The third and final part of the mission is to be an advocate for our seniors in Washington, D.C. We lobby, speak to Congress and push for more funding to allow seniors to stay in their homes. Right now, everything is focused on institutionalization. "Put people in nursing homes, and we'll pay for the nursing home." Nursing homes are necessary. Yes. There are many patients who have to be in a nursing home because of their medical needs.

However, a significant portion of people who are put in nursing homes who would be able to remain at home for far less cost if funding was available. As the Institute takes care of more and more seniors, and our statistics prove that this is a viable, long-term solution, we will be pushing to get more funding from the government to keep people home, so they ultimately can age in place with dignity and grace.

This is our purpose. This is our mission. This is the reason why we established this organization, and therefore all the profits from the purchase of this book will go towards the Institute.

Steve "The Hurricane"™ Weiss

Steve, tell me about your business?

Steve: Home Care Marketing by Hurricane Marketing Enterprises is a business in which we help service providers find those in need of care, and our ultimate goal is to help these service providers increase their revenues and their profits. I started Home Care Marketing in 2012 after working at Care Choice, which was a home care company in central New Jersey. I became vice president after I succeeded in my role as director of business development at Care Choice.

Steve, how did you get into the home health care business?

Steve: I got into the business by accident. I hadn't planned to come into home health care. I went to school to be a minister. I studied theology and as a theology major, every class I took was a religion class or a developmental psych type class like sociology and psychology; all types of social work-related courses.

Having that pastoral training just made me empathetic and understanding of what somebody is going through towards the end of life. Whether they're religious or not, my training really helped me out in my work.

I literally answered an ad on Monster.com looking for a director of business development at a home care company; I was 24 years old at that time.

I say this all the time to my clients, I feel that you don't just get into health care. You're called into health care; whether it's from a higher power or some personal experience. Many people have a situation where their mother or their father had something happen to them and, that's what called them into health care. For me, home care was the perfect balance of my education and my prior work experiences.

How long have you been in business?

Steve: This is my 12th year, and it's just been an amazing run. There are so many people that I've helped directly. There are so many situations that I've come across where I feel if it wasn't for the efforts that we put across in providing the care and coordinating other services, our clients would've been hurt, or they would've been without vital life-sustaining services and they would have suffered. That's what we're trying to avoid. We provide care for our seniors so that they can remain at home to age in place with dignity and grace because that's where they want to be. No one should be in a nursing home. No one should die alone in a hospital. I feel that when that happens it is a tragedy.

I went to school to be a pastor; I currently am a deacon at my church. Scripture is part of my everyday life. I preach once a month. Once every six weeks, I minister to people in nursing homes or pray with people when I travel across the country. Prayer is a daily part of my life, so my professional training comes from both experience and a religion-based practice.

The other side of this was my work experience. I had always had sales and marketing type positions, from the time I was a child. I was raising money for school fundraisers and when was 14 years old, I had my own landscaping business. I had to go out and advertise to get clients. Later, when I was in college, I was selling Cutco knives or working at the dairy selling some type of a product or service. That was my work experience.

As you've mentioned, home health care is a touching business. What's your passion about it that gets you up day after day?

Steve: The passion that keeps me going every single day is the ability to see these seniors and know that what we're doing keeps them home. The phrase "age in place with dignity and grace" is a phrase that I have said many times over the last four or five years. Whether it was out there marketing - going to doctors and nursing homes asking for referrals, asking for patients who needed help, as well as in my role as the owner of Hurricane Marketing Enterprise, in training other home care business owners.

So, it was not easy waking up and driving to these referral sources and asking for business. It was not easy sitting down and meeting with families that had all types of unique situations. These ranged from family dynamics, the pain and suffering the patient himself was going through, the unique chronic conditions and the combination of chronic conditions that the patient herself had, to the living arrangements that patients had. This included whether a patient lives by herself, she lives with her husband, or she lives with one of her children. No two cases were the same.

Being able to help somebody who, a few weeks ago, was independent and healthy and, now, they could be bed-bound. They could have broken their hip. They could have had a stroke. They could have had an injury from a fall, a concussion, a urinary tract infection, pneumonia, diabetic complications, or a combination of all the above. This now causes them to be at a point where they're afraid of dying. It becomes real. They don't know what the next step is. They did not plan for this day and yet it's now happening. The family is blindsided because just last week or just last month, mom was independent. Now, she can't get out of bed. Who's going to be able to help her?

Every day we hear clients say, "I promised my mother I would never let her be in a nursing home. Suddenly, now, this is what I'm faced with." The clients are very motivated, and they need our help. They can't manage their loved one's care on their own. So, my mission--what gets me up every day is knowing I help avoid that decision from having to be made.

I'm helping tens of thousands of people get the care that they need so that they can stay at home and out of our nursing homes. This way, they can age at home with dignity and grace. That's what gets me up each and every day.

Tell me about Hurricane Marketing Enterprises and the types of clients you help.

Steve: Hurricane Marketing Enterprises exists to help service providers find those in need of care. That's our mission statement. We work with hundreds of home care agencies all around the United States and internationally. We train them on how to find the people who have the greatest need, to help their clients avoid hospitalization, help them avoid re-admissions to the hospital, help them avoid being in a nursing home and help them avoid unnecessary pain and suffering because there wasn't care in place.

We train our home care agency owners to get into a relationship with the social workers and the discharge players at skilled nursing facilities, at hospitals, and at rehabilitation centers to help them identify what population should use private home care. Private home care is fee-for-service, so it's not free. However, the cost of one hospitalization is significantly greater than having a caregiver come out a few hours a day, five to seven days a week. This prevents a hospitalization - not to mention unnecessary pain and suffering.

When somebody falls, and they break their hip and they're by themselves, they could lay there on the floor for hours, sometimes days, before they get care. That is an awful situation.

The number one cause of death in the United States for somebody 65 years and older, according to Medicare, is an unintentional fall. That means, the person fell because of some hazard in their home, and by the time they were discovered, the wound from the injury, whether it was bleeding, or a hematoma caused that person to bleed and to die. In some cases, a concussion or a stroke that caused a fall is what killed the person. That's the number one cause of death. It is completely preventable if there's someone in the home.

If you look at the cost of being in a nursing home, which many people have to pay for, the national average, is around $90,000 to $100,000 a year. In assisted living, the national average is around $40,000 / $45,000 a year. Home care is also around $40,000 / $45,000 a year. So, it's in the ballpark of being in an assisted living community, but the patient gets to stay in the comfort of their home, which many of our seniors have lived in for decades.

If somebody has Alzheimer's or dementia, which is a memory impairment, moving that patient from their home into an assisted living community is not in the best interest of that patient because it's an unfamiliar environment. It is going to lead to greater confusion. It's the same cost to bring in a caregiver in for one-on-one care, and keep that person in the comfort of their home that they know and have lived in for decades. So, home care just makes sense.

This is what we do at Hurricane Marketing Enterprises. Not only do we help our agency owners find these patients, we also help them increase the level of care that they're providing. This includes doing things like caregiver training with the rehab facilities and the hospitals and making sure they're doing a thorough needs assessment. We look at what they are paying their caregivers so that their caregivers can have a meaningful work experience but also earn a decent wage at the same time. This is important to ensure that good caregivers are going to provide the excellent care that's necessary to allow a senior to age in place.

Our clients, the agencies, don't have the horror stories of caregivers trying to hurt someone or caregivers stealing from their patients. That doesn't happen to our clients because we make sure that our clients know how to do proper screening and hiring. They are taking care of their caregivers and, then, they're doing everything properly. This includes admission when they're at the hospital, transitioning a patient from rehab to their home, and making sure that they stay home so that they don't end up back in the hospital.

Over the last four or five years, as president and owner of Hurricane Marketing Enterprises, through the hundreds of agencies that we've worked with, we've helped more than 40,000 seniors.

What geographic area do you serve?

Steve: Hurricane Marketing Enterprises has clients in all 50 states.

How many clients do you work with at a time?

Steve: We're working with about 100 active clients that we're coaching right now. Our average client is a home care agency and, I'm going to say that their average client roster is somewhere between 40 to 100 patients.

What are the most common obstacles that prevent your clients from being able to stay in their home and get the care they need?

Steve: Sometimes, it's the client's own will. That's a big one. So many patients feel they don't want to have help and that's what causes them to go in and out of the hospital. Many times, when I go to a patient referral, I would talk to the patient and I would let them know that we're going to do this week to week. So, they're not committing to a long-term service with me. We're going to go week to week. And the patient would respond better, saying, "Ok, we'll try it out."

Then, the hardest part is to get a relationship going between the patient and the caregiver. Once that patient comes home, that first week to two weeks is extremely important for the agency owner and the family to make sure the patient and the caregiver develop a working relationship.

What is a working relationship? It's a routine. We get up at a certain time of the day, we take our meals at a certain time of the day, we take a shower every day at this certain hour, we take our medication at these times of the day, we're going to take our physical therapy exercises at these times of the day, and we're going to go for a walk at these times. I'm going to do some light housekeeping at these times of the day and we're going to run some errands at this time of the day.

Making that schedule is vital for the success of a caregiver-patient relationship. Once they meet one another, once they make that schedule and they start executing that plan, that's how you get the senior to become comfortable with accepting the care long-term. Otherwise, it's, "What's this person doing here? I don't want this person to stay here. I don't need help." Then, they let the help go and unfortunately, they end up back in the hospital and they're starting all over again.

You want to get some level of long-term home care put in place. It must also fit within your budget. The budget may only be for somebody coming in 20 hours a week - somebody coming Monday through Friday for four hours a day, even if it's 9:00 to 1:00. That's a very common shift. The son or daughter who lives locally come by on the weekends and they make sure the person's going to be ok. That's more of an affordable situation where somebody's looking at spending somewhere between $1500 to $2000 a month, which is significantly lower than in an assisted living. It's less than paying for a nursing home. There is no pain and suffering of going through hospitalization. There is still going to be a cost, but it's more affordable than many people realize.

To recap, it's the willingness of the patient to have somebody provide care, and their ability to pay for it. It is making sure that the relationship between the patient and the caregiver is one that works and, then, creating a routine that the patient and the caregiver are going to stick to and follow every single visit.

What would be your advice to the reader who's serious about helping a loved one remain at home with care?

Steve: Start early. Get the care before there's a major episode. When something major happens such as mom falls and breaks her hip, that is a six-month minimum road to recovery. So, the person - mom in that case - goes to the hospital for a couple of days to a week, and she then goes to a rehab facility for about a month. When she comes home, she's going to need help for another three to six months on top of that. Help is going to be required daily, covering all the waking hours. That is about eight to twelve hours a day, seven days a week unless you can physically be there and help with this recovery. That's a long time. And that's a lot of financial resources. That kind of care is going to cost you $1200/$1500 a week with a private care agency.

Could it have been avoided? Could it have been prevented? Possibly, if there was a caregiver in place early on. As soon as mom starts to show a decline, as soon as the physician starts to talk about taking away the keys and the driving privileges, that's when you want to make sure that there's some level of care in place. Don't wait until there is a major episode where it's going to cost you $1000 or more every single week. Get it in place now where the cost is several hundred dollars a week, but the care is long-term. This will help mom avoid ending up in the hospital with a major acute medical episode.

I say mom meaning mom, dad, grandma, grandpa or whoever it is. Get some level in place as soon as the patient starts to decline. Another scenario that should prompt you to start to consider care, even part-time, is if your mother or father suffers from multiple chronic conditions and they live by themselves. If mom and dad are living together, usually the healthier one can provide the help. I do say usually, as you have to watch out for caregiver burnout too.

If dad had a stroke and mom is the primary caregiver, don't let mom take on this responsibility by herself because something might happen to her from burnout. Get somebody who's helping with both of them - at the very least the bathing and toileting assistance for three to four hours a day.

Let's say mom is there to help with more of the companionship. We don't want her trying to lift dad every day because we don't want mom to hurt herself too. That is a worst-case scenario, that you don't want to have happen.

Helping out and getting the care in place before there is a major acute episode is key. Five or more chronic conditions is something you want to look for.

A patient who suffers from five or more chronic conditions is representing 20% of the Medicare population, yet nearly 75% of the billions of dollars that Medicare gets is spent on this minority of the population. So, it's literally 80/20. Eighty percent of the money is going to 20% of the population. Why? Because this percent of the population is constantly in and out of the hospital.

For example, if your loved one has dementia, congestive heart failure, COPD, hypertension, and diabetes, that's an example of somebody who has five chronic conditions. Or they have cancer and any combination of the others they are at risk. If they have a urinary tract infection, they have pneumonia, they have emphysema, they have macular degeneration or any combination of four or five of these conditions increase the likelihood that they are going to end up in the hospital. Dad is going to end up in the hospital if I don't get care and get care in place now. That will prevent unnecessary hospitalizations.

In some instances, even getting care in place, mom may eventually pass away. This is life and death. We're all going to die, so getting care in place and keeping mom at home as long as possible is a win. That's what you want to have happen. If the caregiver shows up one day and mom has passed away overnight, that's a win. Mom never went to the hospital and avoided the associated pain and suffering that many people go through, but she was able to do so at home. Because you were pro-active, you got the care in place and mom could age in place until her last day. That is a huge win. I would rather that happen versus not have care, and mom falls, ends up in the hospital, mom has a stroke, she's in rehab for three or four months and, then, she passes away there. That's a failure.

This proactive approach helps prevent that from happening. Getting care in place early and identify when mom has a need based on how many chronic conditions she has. Get that care going before there's a major episode.

Are there any pitfalls the readers should be aware of?

Steve: Make sure they are going with a legitimate agency. I know it costs more money, but what you're saving by hiring somebody directly or hiring somebody through a dot com, is not worth it. The agency must meet certain criteria to be an agency.

Number one, they must pay the people, so you're not paying the caregiver directly. The agency is responsible for that, which is important because you don't want to have your parent responsible for exchanging money with this caregiver.

The second thing is the agency is responsible in case there's a theft, damages or an injury. If your loved one is hurt because of a caregiver, the agency is responsible for that. Therefore, you want to find out if they have bonding and insurance. Basically, insurance covers an injury whereas bonding covers the theft or something broken in the home. If mom has an expensive set of pearls, which you should not leave in the house anyway, and the caregiver was to steal it, the agency bonding covers that.

The agencies must do a thorough background check on potential caregivers, which means they're not sending criminals into the home. If a criminal somehow slipped through the process, the agency is fully liable for that. So, you know you have a good, wholesome person with a clean-record coming into the home to take care of your loved one.

The other reason why I like the agency is the agency's ultimately the responsible party. They have schedulers, so in the event there is a caregiver that doesn't show up, they should have protocols and procedures in place to make sure someone is there, or alert you right away if there isn't someone coming out. Also, if you don't like the assigned caregiver or you need to change a caregiver, they have other people on their staff that they can send.

Many agencies have nurses on staff. You want to find out if they do because the nurse develops what's called a *plan of care* that the caregiver is going to follow in the home setting. So, when mom is getting the care every single day, every week, it's from a formalized plan of care that was written by a registered nurse. The plan is designed based on mom's unique considerations and limitations. Many agencies will send out this nurse every 60 days, sometimes more frequently depending on the situation or if there's a change in condition.

If mom does go to the hospital but she's not admitted, she's just there for the day and she comes back home, the nurse will come out. Yes, you may have to pay for it, but it's worth it because the nurse will adjust the plan of care based on mom's new condition and the change to her health status. You get that oversight, and that gives you peace of mind knowing that it is not just a caregiver coming in the house, but there's an agency that manages and is responsible for the caregiver coming in.

You want to find an agency that has a caregiver portal, meaning you as a family can access the notes online as to what's going on in the house daily, weekly, and monthly etc. You should have a point person at the agency. They should do random spot check visits. This is why I say go with an agency; these are all things that they do that a caregiver on their own cannot. You've got to interview many agencies because not every agency does this. There are differences between agencies, and it comes down to price. I understand. A couple of dollars an hour more is worth all this peace of mind you get with an agency that does all of these things.

My former agency, Care Choice, did these things. All the agencies that we're working with provide these services or are upgrading the level of care to include them. They are necessary to keep our seniors aging in place with dignity and grace, keeping them out of the hospitals, and out of the nursing homes.

When you're looking for a caregiver, make sure they're from a reputable agency that dots their I's and crosses their T's. Go with the agency that you feel comfortable will get the job done correctly.

What should they look for in choosing someone to help them?

Steve: When it comes to the individual person, the main consideration is there has to be a fit where the patient and the caregiver get along. This is the personality match-up; it is not going to be a one-hit wonder. It is not going to be the case where the first impression is a lasting one. Many times our patients, don't want the care, even though they need it and they understand they need it. But they don't want the care, so it's never going to start out with them saying, "Oh, I love this person," on the first visit. That is very unlikely. Give it four or five visits before trying another person. On that first visit, there's a lot of things that happen. This is why you've got to go with an agency because the agency sets it all up. The good agency has a transition plan to set it up appropriately.

The good agencies will do the following: have the nurse come out, then somebody from the operation comes out with the caregiver to get started. They don't just send somebody into the home. When they come out, they introduce the patient to the caregiver. The nurse will make that formalized plan of care in the home setting with the patient and the caregiver together.

This plan will include going through the medications, going through the routine of when the caregiver's going to do the meal preparation when they're going to help with the medications when they're going to run their errands and all the other things the caregiver is going to do. Then, after they make that formalized plan of care, they're going to inspect the house and make sure there are no safety hazards. This can significantly reduce the likelihood of the patient hurting themselves because of something in the home that is a hazard. Once all that happens, then the caregiver and the patient are going to be left to themselves to start to follow this plan of care. And every day, day one, day two, day three, they're going to follow this plan of care.

By day four or day five, you should get a good sense as to whether this patient and this caregiver are the right match. If it's not the right match, you contact the agency and ask for someone else. It is always good to give it three or four days before making a change. The first day is so much transition and they may not have gotten used to one another yet. By that third or fourth day, they've started to get into a routine, they have started to get to know each other, the caregiver has started to help with the bathing and the toileting, and they are taking them to doctor's appointments and running errands. They have started to execute that plan and they should start to be able to develop a relationship that will lead to a long-lasting one. Always give it three or four days after that initial day of startup.

What's the biggest misconception about home health care?

Steve: The biggest misconception is that you just 'place a caregiver in the house and that's the end of it'. There are agencies out there that do that. Those are not the agencies that you should be choosing. You want the agency that's going to be involved in the care coordination and managing their caregivers and properly managing the situation that you're presented with. So, the biggest misconception is that an agency just places a caregiver in the house and they never touch that client or that patient ever again.

Again, you get what you pay for. If you're looking for a bargain, you're not going to get the good, legitimate agency. The good, legitimate agencies are going to cost a little bit more than your bottom-of-the-barrel companies. But they're going to manage the case, manage the care that's being provided. As a result, you're going to have a positive outcome which is one where mom does not end up in the hospital and she has help for the rest of her life until she eventually passes away in the comfort of her own home.

Is there anything that patients and their families can do to prepare for working with an agency?

Steve: If you can prepare for it, make sure you plan for it financially. If you can get a long-term care insurance policy, that will be beneficial in the long run. They're on the pricey side and many people complain about how much they cost, but when I look at it, a long-term care insurance policy will probably cost about 10% of your entire retirement. You're probably thinking, "Whoa, that's a lot of money," and it is.

One hospitalization where somebody has a stroke--which this happens to Americans all the time - and they have resources meaning they still have retirement funds available, they have no choice but to pay for their medical costs out of pocket. If somebody has $300,000 in retirement savings left when they have this stroke, they're going to have to pay for it out of pocket. This could mean years in a nursing home or years paying for home care where you'll spend down your entire retirement savings on this one condition. Stroke is the number one cause of long-term disability. If the stroke doesn't kill the person, it will take years to get healthy again, if ever. The amount of medical costs would be far greater than the $50,000 to $100,000 that they would spend getting the long-term care insurance policy that will pay for care for the rest of their life.

How can you prepare for it? Make sure that you have the resources available, whether it's home care or any other part of health care--elderly care. It could be assisted living, or it could be adult day care. Those are other services that are available, but they're all fee-for-service.

You do not want to be on Medicaid. Medicaid is government assistance and the care provided is the bottom of the barrel. You get what you get; there is no complaining, there's no arguing. You see people that are forced to move into the nursing homes because Medicaid is going to pay for it. That's the government's solution. The government solution is to move your loved one into a nursing home. If you promised your mother or your father that you would never let them move into a nursing home, don't let them be on Medicaid, because that's what their option will be.

If you can get them to financially plan for their golden years and have that long-term care policy, then it will pay for some of any needed home care. Or you can have Mom and Dad sign over their resources to you so that you manage it early on and manage it well. Be responsible. Then, when they have the need, you can pay for their needs with the money that they gave you. If somebody has a major acute medical episode, they don't have any resources, they're going to be forced to rely on Medicaid and be moved into a nursing home and that's where they're going to spend the rest of their life.

To avoid that, make sure that you plan with financial resources. There are other resources out there. If mom owns a home, you can get a reverse mortgage. A reverse mortgage can be a great thing, but you must look into it.

It's a common misconception that with a reverse mortgage, the bank gets your house. That's a myth. When you do a reverse mortgage, the bank gives you money monthly based on the equity of the house.

In many cases, our seniors across the country own their house outright. If they've lived in their home for 30 to 40 years, it has increased in value. If they bought the house for $30,00 to $50,000 decades ago, that same house is now worth $200,000, $300,000, $400,000 to half a million dollars. So there's equity in that house. The reverse mortgage can get somebody care for five to ten years until they pass away. Then, when the person passes away, you sell the house. After you sell the house, the bank gets back what they paid up front plus a little bit of interest. They get their money back with a small amount of interest. You get to keep the remaining amount. This is a great way for somebody without cash to get long-term funds and be able to pay for services like private home care.

Is there anything else you want to add?

Steve: Other funding sources available are a veterans' program. There are programs out there. You can check with your state to see if there's state funding available. You can search based on the condition your loved one has, to see if there are any supporting organizations that offer funding. Organizations like the Alzheimer's Association and other non-profit organizations offer some kind of funding towards respite care or some level of funding to help prevent caregiver burnout. There are always different things you can do to get funds, so make sure to do some research.

You may want to consider hiring a private geriatric care manager. I like to hire these managers because they do a lot of the care coordination and turning over rocks and stones to find resources and services that are available for the senior.

There are many options and variables, as well as systems to navigate, but I don't expect people to know this. If you don't know this industry, it's like anything else. I'm not a plumber, so when my bathroom had a leak that was dripping into my kitchen, I had to hire a plumber. He had to take out the wall, find the leak, fix the leak and everything else. I don't know how to do that. I had to pay thousands of dollars for an expert to do this, but it was worth it because the leak was fixed, and it was fixed correctly. Now I can use my shower in my bathroom and it's not leaking in my kitchen anymore.

It's the same thing with home care if you don't know this industry, trying to figure it out yourself is going to be problematic. It's worth it to pay a care manager. They cost anywhere from $50 to $150 an hour depending on where you are in the country. it's worth it to pay somebody two or three hours a week to coordinate and manage this care for you because they know what they're doing, and they know where to go and they know how to get these resources for you.

Again, having financial resources is huge at end-of-life, so plan so that you are able to afford these things. Get the right care in place to avoid hospitalizations and nursing home stays.

Case Study - A Married Couple – Wife had a stroke

Clients: Janice and Ken

Scenario:

Ken and Janice were husband and wife. Janice suffered a massive stroke and Ken was in good health. They had to choose between 24/7 home care or nursing home care.

Family and Support:

Some family lived out of state, and the family members who lived nearby were unable to lend much support because they worked full time and had their own children and grandchildren to tend to.

Considerations:

This case required nursing and physical care for Janice and companionship support for Ken. They also required a hospital bed. The caregiver had to be acceptable and compatible with Ken, even more so than with Janice.

Steve: I came to love this family dearly. Janice was usually bed-bound and asleep, and when I did speak with her she was usually not feeling well and not entirely cognitive. I was fortunate enough to get to know her husband Ken and his family.

Here I was, a bright-eyed 24-year-old man, and I had Ken telling me the golden years aren't so golden. Janice, whom Ken had met right after he served in World War II, had worked as a secretary until she retired at 70 years old. She suffered a stroke one month after her retirement party. She abruptly went from enjoying complete independence and travel with her husband to becoming bed-bound. She would never walk again, and her life became a slow wait until death. It was a horrible situation.

Although Ken is a physically large man- and very proud- he couldn't lift Janice out of the bed and assist with everything she needed. Janice needed around-the-clock help, so Ken decided on live-in care. We served Janice for about five years. During that time, we rotated caregivers. I am unsure if the reason was due to relationship or personality compatibility, but a change was requested.

I visited Ken and Janice every month. Ken preferred my team personally come collect the check from his home.

I'll never forget - the first time I met Ken was shortly after I joined the company. The office knew him as the 'collections guy' and Ken had been making payments to our former owner, Ryan, a five-foot-tall, 160-pound man. When I first rang Ken's doorbell, he came to answer, eyes downward as to look for Ryan. Instead, he was met with a six foot two, 230-pound man comprised of six percent body fat and shredded muscle (did I mention muscle?).

He looked up at me and he said, "Son of a gun."

I replied, "What do you mean?"

He said, "That Ryan is one smart man. He's five foot nothing, hundred and nothing pounds, small, Jewish guy. He sends this six foot two, 250-pound linebacker who runs 40 yards in 4.2 seconds to come collect the money."

From that moment forward, I loved Ken. I was a single guy at the time, so I had time to visit on weekends and cook barbeque on the grill. We all ate dinner outside, including Janice and the caregiver. During the holidays, I would see their children and grandchildren. They became surrogate grandparents to me.

I visited the house once a month to collect the bill for their home care, but I wound up staying for hours. Local family members were limited in their abilities but were able to visit their mother about twice a month. Instead of packing in care tasks into one visit, the family was able to spend quality time with Janice and Ken because of our care system.

I cried when Janice passed away. I attended the funeral, greeted the family, and when I walked up to Ken, he gave me a big hug as I offered him my condolences.

He said, "Janice lived a long life and she had a good quality of life in her last years because of the caregivers that you sent into our home. We love you and we look to you as if you were one of our grandchildren. And, so, both Janice and I would be honored if you would be a pallbearer."

"Ken, I would be honored," I told him. I'll never forget it.

The caregiver was kept on shift for several months during Ken's grieving process to help him through the loss. Our caregivers assisted with so much more than Janice's physical needs; it was about the relationship with her husband and family. Eventually, Ken needed help, so we coordinated care until he was eventually laid to rest.

This is why I do what I do. This case is a notable example of how home care makes a difference. Janice was able to stay in the comfort of her own home beside her husband. They slept in the same bed, very little change took place overall, and she got the care she needed. By having a caregiver in place, Janice was able to pass with dignity and grace, and her family was able to maintain a reassured quality of life.

Case Study - A Single Patient Living on Their Own- Didn't want to let go of the finer things in life

Client: Grant

Scenario:

Grant was a 98-year-old single man who suffered a stroke, leaving him partially paralyzed.

Family and Support:

He had no family but had a strong support network made up of his friend Beverly, and other nearby friends and colleagues.

Considerations:

The patient was a tall, broad man, so the caregiver needed to be strong enough to lift him. We only considered male caregivers. We also needed to modify the home to make sure it was a safe environment. This included installation of proper lighting because the old house underwent minimal upkeep in recent years.

Steve: Grant was an amazing individual. I'll never forget—he was a man who fell in love with one person in his lifetime. He served his country during World War II and planned to marry his love, June, but tragedy ended her life before they could marry. Grant remained celibate and never married.

When I met him, Grant was 98 years old and independent. He had been a brilliant educator; a professor of engineering at a prestigious university in New Jersey. He served on the board of advisors for the university's engineering department until he was 78 years old. He invented numerous engineering procedures still used today. Just think of the energy and mind Grant had!

When he was 98 years old, he suffered a stroke leaving him completely paralyzed on one side of his body. He was told he might never walk again. Despite his fear of going home, staying in the nursing home was no longer an option. He had used up his designated time and was given an ultimatum by the rehab center— he was faced with paying out of pocket to live in the New Jersey nursing home (about $110,000 a year) or coordinate 24/7 live-in care back at the house. Live-in care in New Jersey, at the time, cost around $70,000 a year, a much more affordable option he ended up selecting. Having lived by himself for 20 years prior to his stroke, this meant undergoing major adjustments.

I met Grant at the rehab facility and he was extremely concerned and resistant to receive any care.

I told him, "Here's what we can do. We'll try it out week to week. I will bring your caregiver here, to meet with you and do what's called a "caregiver training" where you, your current therapy team and your future-caregiver will work together."

I managed to pair him up with a male, Dean, because Grant was 6' 2" tall and over 200 pounds, and Dean was strong. I didn't feel any of my smaller female caregivers would be physically able to care for such a large man.

Back home in Africa, Dean was a minister. Grant liked this about Dean because he was a man of faith himself. They bonded, and Grant's fears turned to confidence.

After his stroke, Grant was supposed to be on a low-sodium diet, but old habits die hard. He had a TV dinner every night for his entire life until he was in his upper 50s. TV dinners are number one in line for large salt content, chicken is second.

Grant's dear friend Beverly lived a couple of houses over and whenever she came to visit would remind Dean not to give Grant TV dinners. After two weeks in the house, Grant called me to complain. Keep in mind, he loved Dean, loves the help, loves having somebody to keep him company—"But, Steve, you have got to get me my TV dinners. I don't care what Beverly says. I want my TV dinners, damn it."

That's exactly what he said. I told him I would speak with his doctor.

Dr. Hanks told me one-thousand understandable, health-conscious and health-cautious reasons why Grant couldn't have salt.

After letting her lecture me, I said, "Ok, Dr. Hanks, you are correct. Grant should not have TV dinners and he should be on a low-sodium diet. You are right. Now, that being said and with all due respect to you, who are you, me, or anybody to tell this 98-year-old man, who's living at home with a 24-hour caregiver that he can't have his TV dinners? What are we giving him? Five minutes of time in this world?"

The doctored paused and said, "Steve, you tell Grant that I say no, he should not have his TV dinners. He is a 98-year-old man, so if he wants them, it is ultimately his decision. It's 100% on him."

I called Grant and said, "Grant, guess what? Swanson's is on the menu for dinner tonight."

He thanked me.

I told him, "The doctor said no, you can't have it, but if you're going to do it, it's 100% your decision."

He said, "It is my decision and, yes, I'm going to have it. Thank you."

Grant lived to be 104 years old. In retrospect, I think it was the nightly TV dinners that preserved him. That was his happiness.

I believe the best part about this story is how long Grant lived. He was able to regain mobility, was not bed-bound, and was able to live out his days in the comfort of his own home because of live-in care. During his last six years, with Dean by his side at all times – he had a good quality of life.

Case Study - A Single Patient Living on Their Own, Needed Money Management

Client: Chris

Scenario:

Chris was a single man with chronic illnesses and needed ongoing care. Chris' son, Chris Jr., wanted his father to sell the house and move in with him out-of-state. Chris wanted to stay home, but no agency had been able to manage all his caregiving needs and logistics.

Family and Support:

Chris had no support network nearby. Chris Jr. lived 4 hours away, had a demanding job, and a young family.

Considerations:

Simple care logistics were typically handled by local friends or family, but needed organization by our agency. There were no physical obstacles while setting up care.

Steve: Chris was by himself with a mediocre family support system. His wife had died a few years earlier and his son, Chris Jr., lived out-of-state. Chris had recovered from a previous hip replacement, but macular degeneration prevented him from ever driving again. He had five or more chronic conditions and needed help.

Chris Jr. lived in Massachusetts three to four hours away from his dad. He contacted us because the agency he initially hired did a poor job managing his father's case.

Chris Jr. told us that every time he went back to the house, the care wasn't running smoothly. Luckily, he found us through several recommendations.

Chris' situation required live-in attention and a lot of unique dynamics. The caregiver, Jackie, needed to drive. Chris Jr. maintained his father's car from out-of-state, making sure the vehicle was in working order, so Jackie could run errands and take Chris to medical appointments. She would also drive him to the park, making sure to exercise all his interests. Chris eventually began dating a woman in the same 55 plus community.

We had to work out petty cash access. We created a system allowing Jackie to request money from the office whenever she needed to buy Chris' groceries. We had a lockbox where we kept Chris' money. We included this fee in the bill when Chris Jr. paid his invoice. Whether it was $100 or $200 a week for food and fun, Chris was able to stay well fed and active.

If Chris wanted to visit the movie theater, he was required to pay for Jackie's ticket. Jackie gave us the receipts, and we would submit them to Chris Jr. with the next invoice. This was a unique situation for our agency.

We worked with Chris until his passing 18 months after beginning care. Chris was able to live out his life in his home with the proper care he needed while Chris Jr. was able to maintain his busy work schedule and rest assured his dad was well cared for.

After his father's passing, Chris Jr. wrote us a glowing testimonial. He was so happy we were able to manage Chris' money remotely. He was so thrilled his dad was so well cared for by Jackie. Every time he had visited his dad, he would stop by our office just to say hi, thank us, and tell us "Jackie is doing such a great job with Dad. Thank you so much." He was simply ecstatic that he had the right agency on his side.

Bio

Steve "The Hurricane"™ Weiss is a dynamic and entertaining public speaker, known for his expert knowledge in all things sales and marketing. From an early age, Steve has been driven to succeed and excelled across vastly different industries. Steve founded his current company, Hurricane Marketing Enterprises, in 2012 with a goal to help other business owners across the country. In a few short years, he grew it to a seven-figure business and it has been booming ever since.

Steve has sold out Boot Camps and seminars all over the county for years, even attracting attendees from other continents to hear him speak. With more than a decade of knowledge and a knack for "breaking it down" in easy-to-follow steps, he is known as the "Marketing Guru."

Steve's passion is to lead home care business owners on the path to find people in need of their services and convert these prospects into clients. His company's mission statement is to help business owners increase their census, revenue, and profits. Through his programs and presentations, he has guided thousands of individuals to grow their organizations and continues to help them *blow away the competition.*

With his dedication and hard work, Steve has indirectly helped coordinate care for more than 40,000 seniors. Recently, he and co-author Nicole Peretti came together to found the Institute for Dignity and Grace, a non-profit dedicated to helping Seniors remain in the comfort of their home.

On the personal front, Steve is happily married to his beloved wife Susan, father to his three gifts from heaven- Steven, Sydney, and Sienna. He proudly serves as a Deacon, spreading the gospel to all those he comes in contact with.

Steve "The Hurricane"™ Weiss, President and Owner

Hurricane Marketing Enterprises

http://www.homecaremarketing.net/
848-444-9865

Sandra Dougherty

How did you get into the home health care business?

Sandra: I got into the home care business after my experience with my mom. She became ill in late 2000 and was diagnosed with small cell lung cancer, which is terminal. It all happened very fast. Mom went from driving the car one day to me finding her at home close to death two days later! It was terrible, and I really had no idea she was sick! So we started the process that everyone goes through; she went to the ER, then to ICU, then she was lucky enough to graduate to rehab. I visited her every day for four weeks straight. I'll never forget that cold, snowy December day as I made my way to her room past the social worker's office. The social worker asked if I could stop by and see her after my visit. When I did, she told me that my mom would be discharged by the end of the week. I was shocked. There was no way she could go home. I explained the set-up of my mom's home, that I worked all day, etc. How could she go home? The social worker said, "Here are three brochures for three nursing homes in the area. Please go out and visit them and let me know by Thursday so I can make arrangements to place her." I turned and walked toward the hospital elevators and started to cry.

My mom only lived nine more months after the cancer diagnosis. We share some laughs and a lot of tears.

After she passed, and during part of my grieving process, I reflected on what she and I just went through. I thought WOW! There are going to be a lot of people who are going to go through something very similar to what we just did. They're going to need help making decisions during a really overwhelming time. I thought maybe I can help them.

Six months after her passing I became more serious about learning how I could help people who will need help caring for a loved one. I started making a list of all my questions, like how do you run a background check on someone? How do I find people that need the help? And so on.

By the grace of God, I was blessed with an e-mail at work that came in, regarding home care. As I read on I noticed a small highlighted area at the bottom of the page. It said, "Interested in owning a franchise?" Of course, I clicked on the button in the corner, and six months later I owned a franchise.

How long have you been in business?

Sandra: Twelve years now. I opened the doors on July 1st, 2005. I started training with the national home care franchise I signed on in June of 2005 and then came home and got right on it.

What is your professional background and training?

Sandra: I have a Bachelor's in business administration with a major in finance, and was a financial planner for 17 years before getting into this field. My main area of focus was retirement and long-term care planning. I was fortunate to know what ADL's (activities of daily living) were and how they affect long-term care policies, but that's about it!

Home health care is a really touching business. What is your passion about it that gets you up day after day?

Sandra: It really gets back to my mom, and being able to help people. I'm a problem solver. I like to help people solve problems. And this arena allows me so many ways to help people not only live at home but actually thrive in their homes. Most people don't know that a physical therapist can come to your home and help you get stronger at home. Or that you can combine services like home care with adult day care or other activities to help keep people engaged in the community. We even work to coordinate with palliative and hospice care to provide comfort to the client and their family. It's a really rewarding opportunity to serve people in such a personal way.

Tell me about your agency and the types of clients you help.

Sandra: We help everyone: from "Driving Miss Daisy," to hospice cases where people are going home to spend some of their last days, and everything in between. We can help them with personal care, bathing, laundry, meal preparation, errands, take them to appointments, all the daily activities of living and joyful companionship!

What's the geographic area that you serve?

Sandra: We service all of Stark County, Ohio which is: Canton, Massillon, Louisville, and also Uniontown and Green.

How many patients do you work with at a time?

Sandra: On average, about 120 to 150 people a year.

What are the most common obstacles that prevent your clients from being able to stay in their home and get the care they need?

Sandra: The main obstacle for many people is money. Second is the actual support of the surrounding family because it does take a village to keep somebody at home. We're a big help — We can be in the home 24/7, with aides around the clock — but there are critical decisions that really only family can make. We have to have a good relationship with the family and work together, and sometimes that becomes overwhelming for people.

What would be your advice to the reader who is serious about helping a loved one remain at home with care?

Sandra: People should do their homework. And as early as possible! If your parents or loved one is getting up there, start having those conversations. Do they want to stay home? If so, start asking any of your friends if they have dealt with this yet and who they would recommend. A referral from a friend is a great start. Make some calls and do some shopping of prices. Also, ask if they are bonded and insured, how do they background check their employees, if a caregiver calls off do they send a replacement?

We try to hold informational workshops and have a speaker come to talk about topics like Veteran's benefits for long-term care. Attorney's come in a discuss Medicaid benefits and spend down. We have even had a reverse mortgage specialist and home modification specialist come in to talk. My office is trying to get the information out to people in our community.

Don't' wait until its 3 days before discharge. You don't want to make lifelong decisions in that short a period of time. Start now!

Are there any pitfalls that the reader should be aware of? And what should they look for in choosing someone to help them?

Sandra: If you're picking an agency, do your research. Check the Better Business Bureau for any complaints. You can see if they have used Home Care Pulse: they are a third-party survey company, and they post all kinds of data retrieved from surveys that our clients and caregivers have given. Ask people that you know for referrals or recommendations, so that way you have something a little bit more than just picking up the phone book or looking on the Internet and googling "home care." So, if you know somebody who can give you a recommendation of a good home care agency, that's a good start. Ask "if my caregiver calls in sick am I still going to get service, or am I not going to get service that day?" Questions like that. "How long have you been in business?" And maybe, "How many caregivers do you have?"

You can even ask the agency for references. I love giving my clients the opportunity to brag about us to potential new clients!

What is the biggest misconception about home care?

Sandra: Having a stranger in their home is scary. I always tell them they will be surprised how quickly they will like the person and enjoy having them help around the house. Women are the hardest. We serve a generation where the women did everything. It's hard for them to give this work up to another person especially another woman! We always encourage our aides to keep the lady of the house engaged. It's still her castle!

Is there anything that patients and their families can do to prepare for working with you?

Sandra: Just call. Get a conversation started. We can come out, sit down and do a free assessment. There is no pressure to start with us. We want you to be confident in your choice so that you are with us for a long time!

Be prepared to be honest, as we are going to ask a lot of personal questions about health and personal care. This is an intimate relationship.

Is there anything else you'd like to add?

Sandra: I always tell people that home care is a great idea. It's an awesome option. They need to be realistic and know that it's not going to be perfect. It's a people business and people aren't perfect. We make mistakes, but we are willing to work hard to fix them and give you the best possible service available.

For my office, our mission, our goal, is to never, ever have a shift missed. You are still going to have a caregiver even if your original caregiver calls off.

Case Study – Single, Retired Military Man, Immobilized by Stroke

Client: Edward [Ed]

Scenario: Ed is a 65-year-old single male, living alone who suffered a stroke.

Family and Support:

Ed has one sister who works fulltime, and a mother who needs care herself. This is not an ideal support system.

Considerations:

Ed's right side is compromised because of stroke complications, and he is aphasic, which means he can't speak. He needed accommodations to continue living in his home.

Sandra: Ed was in his late 50's when he suffered a severe stroke in 2008. He was newly retired, having served in the Pentagon for 25 years, and returned to his hometown after purchasing a two-story colonial for refurbishing. He has one sister and his mother lives alone. His support system is really nominal because his mother needs care and he never married. The stroke affects his full ability to speak and absorb conversation. He has aphasia, so it was difficult for him to safely navigate the home.

We worked with a home healthcare agency that offered physical therapy, occupational therapy, and a nurse. We helped him up and down stairs and around the home. We assisted for three years when he finally decided to downsize. He didn't love the idea, but it was the right thing to do. Due to his complications, we've pretty much remained his 24/7 primary caregivers.

There were obstacles in setting up care. Set-up is the biggest challenge. For instance, you have options to transform a regular shower into a safer shower. You can install a hand-held shower head or a bench. Grab bars are always helpful. He was able to get a lot stronger despite immobility of his right side. After a stroke, there's a lot of pain on the affected side. The caregivers had to learn how to dress him without aggravating the pain. There is a proper way to dress somebody after they've been debilitated. In that home, the stairs were the worst obstacle. We were able to go to the grocery store, make meals, do laundry, clean the house and help him with personal hygiene.

Ed lives about as independently as anybody I've ever known with his situation. He's had a couple complications with cancer. We always tell him he's the cat with nine lives. He keeps bouncing back and the first thing he and his caregivers do is hop in the car and hit the town.

He likes to go to this little coffee shop and run errands. He has a cat now, so he has a small companion that we help take care of. The caregivers prep Ed's food and place the meals into little containers so it's easier for him to warm in the microwave. They'll also cut the food beforehand since he can't use his right side to hold a fork or knife.

He has such a great family. We ended up taking care of his mom for a little bit. I think his sister would tell you, if there's anything she can rely on, it is our agency. She's written that compliment in a couple surveys. She wouldn't know what to do if it wasn't for us being there to help Ed. It enables her to do all the other things she needs to do in her life as well.

Case Study – Combative Dementia patient, Wife with Limited Mobility

Client: Ricky and Mary

Scenario:

Ricky is currently 77 years old and Mary is 82

Family and Support:

The couple's children do live nearby, but they are raising families of their own. Providing care for their parents poses an obstacle in their busy daily life.

Considerations:

Ricky has dementia and can become combative. Mary has spinal stenosis and a broken ankle. Despite their ailments, they are very independent. Mary can be very demanding, and it took her and her husband a while to get used to having caretakers in their home.

Sandra: Ricky and Mary raised their family on a farm. If you happen to know any farmers, you would know the wives are a very strong breed of woman and very independent. While Ricky ran the farm, Mary took care of the home and raised the kids. They're both very strong-willed people.

We began service in March of 2014. Ricky had dementia, which then progressed into Alzheimer's — and a very combative Alzheimer's at that. He could be very verbally and physically tough on the caregivers, but the gals were always good with him and very attentive. He's been bed-bound for probably four or five months now, but he's still feisty as ever.

Mary already had spinal stenosis, which I believe she suffered from most of her life. It may have been a birth defect, but regardless, it became progressively worse. She also broke her ankle. She was doubly compromised and needed help.

Overall, Mary had a good recovery. We just took her out to our Christmas party and she had a blast.

My team is there for them. I think even when Ricky passes we'll continue to be there for Mary. She's grown accustomed to the girls being there for care and companionship, so the situation has turned out to be a pretty cool and positive thing.

Bio

Sandra S. Dougherty was born in 1964 to John and Helen Scredon in Canton, OH. Her parents were first-generation Romanian Americans and her father was a Veteran of World War II. Long before she ever thought she would own and operate an in-home care agency, her grandmother was a live-in caregiver for several years.

Sandra went on to finish her college education at the University of Akron completing a BSBA, Finance degree and enjoyed a 17-year long career as a financial planner. In November of 2000, that all changed when she found her mother nearly dead in her home. After getting her to the hospital and having surgery to repair what appeared to be a brain bleed, her mother was diagnosed with small cell lung cancer that had already moved to the brain.

Her mother's diagnosis was terminal, and she was given 3 months to live. After daily visits to her mother, the social worker called her into her office one cold and snowy December day and told her that her mother was being discharged in 3 days.

Shocked and mortified she took the 3 brochures for nursing homes that were given to her. Not having many choices in 2001, Sandra visited each place and found the Inn at Belden, an assisted living facility, as her mother's new home. Her mother lived 8 months from diagnosis to death.

After her experience, Sandra swore that she would do everything could to help people better navigate these waters. After several years of looking and researching, God placed the home care agency opportunity at her feet. She listened, and the rest is history. 12 years later, Sandra owns the most successful and well respected in-home care agencies in her hometown. Her dedication and passion to make this very overwhelming time in a family's life better and easier is her memorial to her loving parents; John and Helen Scredon.

Sandra S. Dougherty

http://www.visitingangels.com/canton/home

330-497-5995

Krista Gaul

How long have you been in home health care, and how did you get into it?

Krista: I've been involved in home health for approximately 12 years. Prior to that, I was working in banking at MBNA America and had taken a severance package from them in 2005. At that time, I called it my "cosmic kick in the ass," because I was trying to figure out what I wanted to do when I grew up. Right around that time my mother, who was perfectly healthy, tripped, fell, and broke her arm and tore her rotator cuff. Because I was not working, I would go to her home every day and try to help her. My mom is a very proud woman, so it quickly became obvious she didn't want my help even though she needed it. She struggled getting dressed, going to the bathroom; those types of things. I tried to hire an agency but after observing the caregivers that were sent to her I thought: this is a basic and fundamental service that people in the community obviously need. I can do this as a business. I have a passion for people, I truly care about the well-being of people, and I certainly can do this better than the agency that I just tried to hire. So, I ended up buying into a franchise in 2005 and have never looked back. My mom was my very first client, and she's still a client today.

You mentioned this a little bit, but I'll just ask: what is your professional background and training?

Krista: I didn't have any home health or healthcare experience when I started. I was in banking for approximately 15 years before I went into home care. The one thing I learned at MBNA was how to provide an incredible customer service experience. My strength in owning a business is thinking about it from a customer perspective, trying to always better our communication, better our performance, raise our standards and increase customer satisfaction. Believe it or not, I learned that from a credit card company. I knew nothing about home health care or anything of the sort; I just jumped in.

Home health care is a touching business. What's your passion about it that gets you up day after day?

Krista: The great thing about being a small home care business is that you can see the direct positive impact that you have on your clients' lives every single day. At least once a week, we will get a call from a family member, or a social worker, or even a referral source, saying, "Thank God you do what you do. Thank goodness you're there." And for me, that's what it's all about. It's not about the money, it's not about the title or accolades; it's about knowing in my heart what I'm doing is genuinely bettering the population of people I'm working with, and I'm hopefully leaving this world a little bit better than I found it.

Tell me about Macklyn Home Care and the types of clients you help.

Krista: I started my business in 2005 and re-branded in 2015. We aren't even two years old since the re-brand and we've grown immensely. We have approximately 100 clients, about 75 to 100 caregivers, and seven office staff. We just opened our second location in Georgetown, Delaware so we can now serve the entire state. Our reputation is preceding us, and as a result, we have grown all of this essentially by word of mouth.

You just mentioned Delaware. Is that your geographic area?

Krista: Yes, we have 2 office locations to serve the entire state of Delaware.

About how many patients do you work with at a time?

Krista: Right now, we have approximately 100 clients.

What are the most common obstacles that prevent your clients from being able to stay in their home and get the care they need?

Krista: The most common obstacle, I would say, is the inability or unwillingness of our clients to install or implement assistive technology or home modifications. Usually, this is a financial decision in that they are not willing or able to spend the money to make those modifications, for example: to widen the doors to accommodate a wheelchair or install grab bars to make a bathroom safer. Sometimes they've simply waited too long and let the situation go too far, and now they don't have the financial resources to implement any of those changes. And without them, the home is not a safe environment to live in. And if the home environment isn't safe, families are forced to consider a facility for their loved one.

What would your advice be to the reader who is serious about helping a loved one remain at home with care?

Krista: Preplan. If you want to stay in your home, or you know your parents want to stay in their home, start planning for that as soon as possible. Maybe that means moving to a one-story home. Maybe that means widening existing doorways. Maybe it means installing grab bars or a stair lift; especially if someone has been diagnosed with a degenerative disease and they know they may eventually need assistive technology. Start making those modifications early so you're not panicked asking last-minute questions like, "How do I make these changes and afford home care and afford medication and transportation?"

I also recommend having those conversations when someone is in the beginning stages of a disease or illness. Especially with dementia, we find way better outcomes when the person with dementia is included in the decision to introduce a caregiver, versus waiting until the illness has progressed to the point where they don't even recognize their own family. If they're not accepting care from family, and now the family is trying to hire a stranger to help them… they will definitely be resistant. Think about that, you and I are healthy, and we don't want a stranger showing up at our door and saying, "Okay, take your clothes off, I'm going to give you a bath now." With dementia, that's their mindset every single day. A stranger showing up: that's awful. Nobody would want that. But if you can introduce the person before their memory is too far gone, or before they are physically compromised, then you're talking about a much less contentious situation because you have a willing participant at that point.

Are there any pitfalls that readers should be aware of? What should they look for in choosing someone to help them?

Krista: Follow-up is critical. You can call any home care company and you'll have a great conversation about what they can provide, what they can do, and how they can go about doing that. They'll try to sell you anything you want to hear over the phone. The important thing to consider is: What's the follow-up after that? How easy is it to get the important people on the phone when you have an issue? What happens if you have an issue overnight, or on the weekends, or on holiday? Is someone still available? Are they still as willing to help you when those crises occur? I think that's the difference between a big agency and a small agency. With a small business, you can get right to the owner of the business, or at least a director level, at any time: weekends, nights, and holidays. Regarding bigger businesses, there are more levels of management, and it's more difficult to get to someone who can have an impact at night or on the weekends — and unfortunately, that's usually when you need somebody. Simply stated: do your research. Talk to the company a couple of times. See how flexible they are in terms of offering solutions to your family's crisis and what their challenges are. See how willing they are to work with you to try to make it work for the family, not what works best for the agency.

What's the biggest misconception about home health care?

Krista: The first thing I always hear is it's too expensive. Ironically, I usually hear that before they even ask me what my prices are. There are usually several options available to assist financially.

Most agencies — I know ours does — will offer some type of flexibility to help accommodate your needs. We offer shifts as small as a one-hour, which a lot of agencies don't. Most agencies have a minimum of a four-hour shifts, and that's great if you need four hours of care. But what if you just need someone to run to pick up a prescription for you? Or what if you just need someone to come and prepare a meal for you because you're recovering from a surgery? You can't do it; you only need an hour, you shouldn't have to pay for four. So, we offer one-hour shifts. We also do split shifts because you might not need somebody sitting with your loved one for eight straight hours a day. Maybe they only need assistance in the morning, at lunch, and/ or in the evening to prepare meals and check in to make sure they're okay.

That's a significant cost saving from when you have somebody there all-day long. We also contract with the Veterans Association to utilize the Aid and Attendant benefit for our clients. And Medicaid offers a Community Based program that pays for non-medical home care services. We utilize as many resources and creative options as we can to help families with cost-effective solutions.

Is there anything that patients and their families can do to prepare for working with you?

Krista: I would just say, again, getting the patient involved in the process as early as possible to get their acceptance. Sometimes that means talking to the children to make the point that there will come a time when they'll need to step in and help. It will be better if that's implemented sooner rather than later.

Is there anything else you want to add?

Krista: That's kind of a loaded question because I can talk all day about what I do, why I do it, and how we do it because it is something that I'm so passionate about.

I think it's important to focus on hiring people that truly care about other people. That's our strength as a company. You can have many titles and credentials behind your name, but if I sit across the table from you, interviewing you, I need to feel like you're in it for the right reasons, that you will genuinely care for my client's wellbeing. If I wouldn't send you into my own parents' home, I won't hire you. I think it's critical in this industry to have high employee standards as our clients are some of the most vulnerable.

Case Study – Senior taken advantage of by own relatives

Scenario: Relatives move into Vicky's home and take advantage of her Medicaid without providing care.

Family and Support: Children or extended family members are present, but not offering support. The family is a detriment because they drain the household's resources.

Considerations: Assuming the family member has moved in with Vicky in order to assist her, Medicaid may reduce support when they perceive family is present. The agency must discern what is actually taking place in the household and advocate on behalf of the patient, so they are not denied care, medication, or resources.

Krista:

It's interesting—since 2005, there has been an influx of otherwise "independent family members" now moving "back in." I feel like the families have good intentions, suggesting and encouraging the newly homeless relative (typically a grandchild) to "move in with Grandma because she's living alone and probably could use the help!"

I observe this more and more. A family member needs a place to live and grandma has a home that she lives in alone. The family member has no intention of providing personal care to grandma and is just looking for a free place to live. Because there is now family living in the home with her, the Medicaid Case Manager assumes the family member is assisting with care for the senior in need. Unfortunately, that isn't the case.

I'll tell the story of, what was then, a unique account. Vicky was living alone. She received Medicaid's services and a caregiver was helping her with multiple shifts daily. Suddenly, her grandson moves in. A case manager from Medicaid came out and surmised that because there was an able family member living with Vicky, they could decrease care hours. In fact, Vicky's grandson slowly drained her of her medical resources, food, and money. The grandson doesn't pay rent under the assumption that Vicky has Medicaid and it's all paid for. Her grandchild views it as a free ride. The only one who suffers is Vicky. It is absolutely heartbreaking to see.

It's our duty, to step in and advocate for the client, trying to regain hours of needed care. We tell Medicaid the family member is unwilling and grossly underqualified to administer personal care. Fortunately, we have successfully fought to correct this situation for our clients.

I believe the family genuinely means well when they implement a new living situation. The intention is in favor of the senior, but the execution is not very well thought out. Recently, I needed a caregiver at Vicky's home at 10:00 p.m. because she was being discharged from the hospital. There were four capable adults living in the house with her, but my caregiver had to be there to escort her back in, get her situated and changed for bed. No one in the family was willing to help because it was too late at night for them.

Case Study – Proud Couple, Husband can no longer care for wife and himself

Client: Krista's mother and father, Scenario:

Mom is a proud Italian woman. Dad's health is worsening.

Family and Support:

Dad is no longer Mom's primary caregiver because of his declining health. Krista's brother lives far away.

Considerations: Krista's mother denies her need for assistance. After her dad was injured, both he and her mom were placed in separate skilled facilities. Krista has children of her own, including a special needs child. She must balance the needs of her career, children, and parents.

Krista: I will tell you my mom's story. My mom was the first client who ordered the caregiver out of her home and told us, "I don't need care. I don't need this person. I'm fine."

She expressed this every day for about a week. So, when people recount to me how their mom or dad resists home care, I understand it on a personal level. Despite the push-back, I eventually chose the right person, and she is still with my mom to this day. When I had just started my home care business, my mom was a client but with infrequent visits (I'm pretty sure my parents didn't trust me yet.) and my dad was her primary caregiver. When my dad had to leave the country for work, my mom agreed to increase the hours and the schedule became more consistent. Only then did she trust the process and the structure I had put into place. We switched gears and had her caregiver come to the house three times a day, seven days a week. That schedule still fluctuates to this day depending on the need.

My mom's health has deteriorated over the years, and now my dad's has too. In fact, last year both were admitted into separate skilled facilities at the same time. My father had been flying a drone plane when he fell down an embankment, broke his foot, and was admitted to a rehab facility for recovery. While he was in the facility, my mom, who was then home alone, fell in the middle of the night and broke her hip. At the time, she had a daytime caregiver who found her on the floor the following day after the incident.

My parents ended up in two separate skilled nursing facilities; traveling back and forth to visit proved slightly difficult. Consider in addition to these check-ups, I had young kids and a job to balance, so I can absolutely relate to the children of seniors who contact me for assistance.

My parents eventually returned home from their respective facilities, but my father, who initially helped take care of my mom alongside the caregivers, is still not 100 percent. We've had to once again increase the amount of times the caregiver visits the house.

Bio

Krista Gaul tells the story of how she essentially "stumbled" into the Home Health field after her mother fell and broke her arm. The need for help was there. And resources seemed slim.

But, the seed was planted 23 years ago. When Krista's sister, just 31 years old, was diagnosed with Osteosarcoma. Within only 10 short months from diagnosis to her passing, Krista's family desperately sought resources to support her and her children -whose ages were 1 and 3 years old. But resources were limited and difficult to find. It left her family with a feeling of sheer helplessness which haunted her for years.

A couple of years later, Krista began working at the credit card company MBNA America. It was an amazing company with very strong core values. And although she wasn't a banker in her heart, she learned several valuable business skills there. The most impact on her came from the company's community involvement which held a strong message: be altruistic in nature; give back to your community and help take care of those who cannot take care of themselves.

So, once again, in 2005, when the need once again arose to help a family member, Krista jumped on it determined to successfully find a resolution this time. But the need to find quality care at an affordable price didn't seem readily available, so she created it herself.

That was 12 years ago, and while the name of the business has changed – the message remains constant. Treat employees with dignity, respect, and fairness – they are the cog in our wheel. Give them meaningful work to do. Set expectations high. Show praise often.

Macklyn Home Care has a responsibility to their Clients to provide the best possible care available. It's a responsibility that is taken very seriously. It's a 24/7 commitment. With flexible schedules and pricing, the goal is to make quality home care affordable – to everyone.

Krista Gaul

www.macklynhomecare.net

302-691-3217

info@macklynhomecare.net

Lynn Marie Houghton, RN, BSN

How long have you been in home care, and how did you get into it?

Lynn: It was 10 years in March of this year, that I started my business. I had just moved to the Lehigh Valley from the Philadelphia suburbs where I grew up; Havertown, Pennsylvania. I read about starting a home care agency in my nursing magazine and I felt there was a strong need for this in our community at that time and the foreseeable future and I knew I had the right skills as a nurse and the head and heart to make this a reality. You could say, "The rest is history!"

What's your professional background and training?

Lynn: I have been a registered nurse since 1989; earning my nursing license from Delaware County Community College and my BSN at Widener University in 2000. My first nursing job was as a staff nurse in a step-down unit from intensive care at Delaware County Memorial Hospital.

The next job in my career was a position as a visiting nurse for the Main Line Health System's home care agency, where I worked for a number of years before I was offered a position as a case manager in their central intake department. I later transitioned to a case management position at Lankenau Hospital (Now Lankenau Medical Center).

I recently worked part-time at St. Luke's Hospital, here in the Lehigh Valley as a Case Manager. Case management is very different than it was 20 years ago; there is much more of a team approach, and everybody works together to help get patients discharged safely home.

Home care is a touching business. What's your passion about it that gets you up day after day?

Lynn: The starting of my home care agency is my tribute to my grandparents. I feel very fortunate that I had them in my life for 35 years. They were a huge part of my upbringing and they helped make me the woman I am today. They lived nearby and shared every holiday and birthday and all their love with my sisters and I, as we were their only grandchildren.

As my grandparents got older and needed more and more assistance, my parents turned to me for help and even though I was a nurse, I was not sure how to guide them. We all just didn't know what to do or where to begin.

My father's mother, my Oma, wasn't eating properly and became confused, weak and unsteady and so we felt we needed to place her in a nursing facility. She was 92 years old and quite healthy but within 2 months of her moving to the facility, she was admitted to the hospital in hypertensive crisis and died two days after she was discharged.

Her death occurred one month before my first son was born, and quite frankly I was, heartbroken and felt an amazing sense of guilt. I had wanted so much for her to be able to meet and hold my first son...I felt that I had let her down when she needed me most!

My mother's parents, my Nan and Pop, were also in need of additional assistance and we moved them to a Continued Care Community where they lived in an apartment in assisted living.

My pop was the caregiver for my nan who had advanced dementia. When my pop became ill and needed to be hospitalized, my nan had to be moved to the nursing home section of the facility because she could not live there on her own.

She never made it out of the nursing home section as she had lost so much weight and had become very debilitated and frail. Sadly, she died on their 65th wedding anniversary. My grandfather died 19 days later. They both died only one year after my oma's death. This was just another immeasurable loss for our family when we thought we had made the best choices for them.

I truly believe in my heart that my grandparents would have lived longer if they had remained living in their own homes with the help of caregivers. It all seemed so complicated at the time and the decisions that my family made were indeed out of love! I also know now that the lack of family planning led to the decisions that were made.

I want seniors and children of seniors to know that remaining in your own home is a real possibility. For many years now, people have been placed in nursing homes when that is not truly where they belong. Homecare has become the new alternative to nursing home care. My hope and personal mission is to help seniors and their families find answers that I was unable to find for three truly special people 17 years ago. I try every day to accomplish this through my work as owner of a home care agency.

A valuable point that I want readers to take from this book is that they need to sit down with their parents or grandparents and plan for their futures. Please don't wait until you are in a time of crisis to make a life-changing decision for your loved ones!

Tell me about your company. What type of clients do you help?

Lynn: The clients we work with have individual needs and we make sure that we design an individual care plan to meet each of their needs. Some persons will need a little help while others need a lot of help or constant supervision. Many clients also are being treated for multiple diseases that affect their ability to perform their normal activities of daily living. Activities such as bathing and dressing, using the bathroom, preparing and eating meals, shopping, housework, laundry, taking their medications on time and even walking and transferring from a seated to a standing position, or into and out of a car or bathtub. Clients who have dementia are sometimes unable to make appropriate decisions for themselves regarding personal care and safety.

Our agency helps with all of these activities while allowing the person to be as independent as possible as well as maintain their dignity. Most seniors are devastated by not being able to drive anymore. This is why, we also provide transportation which comes with companionship. Safety is of utmost importance in our care!

What geographic area do you serve?

Lynn: We service the entire Lehigh Valley including Northampton and Lehigh Counties as well as a small part of Bucks County in the state of Pennsylvania; which includes both city and rural areas!

How many clients do you work with at a time?

Lynn: We presently have close to 200 clients and provide service to more than 80 active (and growing every week) on a regular weekly basis.

What are the most common obstacles that prevent your clients from being able to stay in their home and get the care they need?

Lynn: A very frustrating obstacle is that most people do not even know that there are private agencies available that will provide assistance for the elderly in their own homes. These are services that will give peace of mind to adult children when they are working because they know their loved one is safe and being taken care of when they cannot be there.

The hospital case managers, rehabilitation social workers, and discharge planners, as well as physician offices; need to educate their patients about the private duty home care services that are readily available in their communities. If they don't, they become the obstacle.

Another obstacle is that people think they cannot afford assistance in the home. I would ask them, "Can you afford to not have the assistance? Can you afford the costs of being hospitalized? Can you afford to fracture a hip?" Many seniors are commonly hospitalized as a result of a fall because of an unsafe environment or dehydration due to poor intake, or a urinary tract infection that goes untreated due to improper personal care or a skin tear that becomes infected.

In addition, most people don't realize Medicare recipients are responsible for 20% of the hospital and rehab bill if they do not have a secondary insurance. Readmissions to the hospital within 10 days are common for older adults due to medication errors, falls and not following up with their physician as directed. These elderly persons are transitioning from an environment where they are being helped with everything from bathing, meal preparation, medication delivery and therapy exercises to zero help. Idealistically, can they safely go home alone? And don't forget the hospital billing process starts all over again when they are re-admitted. Statistics show that falls are the leading cause of injuries in older adults and that persons who fracture their hips may never fully recover and that may lead to death or dependent care. (CDC.gov)

People are living longer, and many have the presence of multiple disease symptoms that they are under medical supervision for, and they NEED assistance in the home to help them to remain safe whether they realize it or not. The reality is that a helping hand at home can mean the difference between staying at home or requiring dependent care in a facility for the rest of one's life.

One adult child alone may not be able to afford for care at home for their parent but if they combine their monies together they will find services very affordable and can relieve them of many of the duties they do not have the time to do but feel they are obligated to help with. They will no longer need to run over to their parent's home after work when they feel dead tired or when they receive an emergency phone call from them in the middle of the night or while at work. They will also find that they can spend quality time together.

What would be your advice to the reader who's serious about helping a loved one remain at home with care?

Lynn: Adult children need to help their parents prepare in advance for their "Golden Years". If they wait until a crisis occurs it may be too late. As I already stated, a fall with a fractured hip can lead to dependent care and sometimes death!

Adult children should be visiting and checking in on their parents regularly; weekly if they are able. This gives them an opportunity to assess the state of the house; check the food in the refrigerator, evaluate if medications are being taken properly, take notice of incontinence odors, assess cleanliness and safety. Specifically, take notice of rotting and outdated foods. Count pills in the bottle to see if the correct number have been taken since last filled. Take notice of what your parents are wearing and check laundry baskets for clothing as persons with memory issues tend to re-wear dirty clothing. Check showers to see if they are cluttered with items being stored and if they contain soap and shampoo (parents may tell their children they are taking showers when they really are not). Check the parent's car for any dents and dings which may trigger the question of whether they are safe to drive, even if it is "just locally". Check the home for loose throw-rugs and other tripping hazards as well as the need for handrails, grab bars in the bathroom and raised toilet seats. Is their parent safe carrying a basket of laundry up and down the basement steps?

When the adult child sees a need for assistance they need to sit down with their parent and siblings to have a frank discussion about concerns and needs. A simple solution can be bringing in a caregiver to help daily or a few times a week.

Many older persons are socially isolated so not only will they be receiving help to keep them safe, they also will have a companion to talk and share with. If the adult child feels their parent is not safe to live alone without help, or that they need assistance with certain chores, they need to be adamant with their parents when having this discussion. If certain precautions are not taken their loved one can be injured or hospitalized as a result and the situation may then turn into a crisis. No one wants to admit they need help, but I am certain they would rather get some help from a caring individual than lose their home.

Are there any pitfalls that the reader should be aware of? As in, what should they look for in choosing someone to help them?

Lynn: Believe me when I say, not all home care agencies are the same! You should consider more than pricing when deciding on a home care agency for your loved one. People in need should look for a reputable home care agency who has caring, knowledgeable and dedicated staff. Ask if the agency has any specialty programs to meet your parent's needs and if their caregivers are compassionate and reliable. A home care agency should go above and beyond to make sure your loved one is well-taken care of by hiring compassionate, reliable caregivers and by communicating with you regularly about your loved one's care. Don't be afraid to ask for a copy of their license and insurance information. The company should be licensed (in most states they must be licensed) bonded and insured. Please keep in mind that in this life, you get what you pay for. Many people hire home care agencies based on price alone but not what really matters, the care team!

The local county Area Agency on Aging (AAA) will also have a list of local home care agencies. They should reach out to their physician's office, case managers in the hospital and social workers in rehabilitation facilities to find the names of reputable agencies. Word of mouth is a great way to find a good agency. If you hear someone is bragging about how happy their parents are with a home care agency, write the name down and call them to gather more information.

What's the biggest misconception about home care?

Lynn: The greatest misconception is that Medicare covers all needs. Medicare only covers medical care in the home after a hospitalization. These services are provided by Home Health Care Agencies. They provide visiting nurses, physical, occupational and speech therapist. Medicare does not cover private duty care. This service is provided by a Home Care Agency. The names are close but provide two different services. Private duty home care is paid for privately but also can be paid for by long-term care insurance, Veteran's Aid and Attendance programs, and through local counties Area Agency on Aging. Please note that veteran and public assistance are determined by income.

Another misconception about home care is that hospice is a place that persons go to die. There are indeed hospices for persons that are actively dying but in-home care hospice relates to "a philosophy of care". A person must decide that he no longer wants to return to the hospital for medical treatment but wants to die peacefully in their home. A physician must write an order that the person has less than 6 months to live.

The hospice care includes visiting nurses, social workers, home health aides, a chaplain and volunteers who serve as a team to help keep the individual comfortably at home but does not include 24-hour care. Typically, families hire homecare agencies for 24-hours or as needed. Hospice is misconstrued as a scary word because people associate it with death, but persons can be under hospice care for many years and live comfortable, happy lives. Only God knows when it is someone's time to leave this earth!

Is there anything the seniors and their families can do to prepare for working with you?

Safety, safety, safety! They should make sure that their home environment is a safe one. If the elderly person is having difficulty walking up and down stairs, then a first-floor setup should be considered. Get rid of the dining room set and make a bedroom. If there is no bathroom downstairs, add one or use a commode. A hired caregiver can assist with cleaning, meal preparation, and personal care needs.

As I mentioned earlier, add handrails and grab bars if needed. Buy a raised toilet seat and shower chair for safety because most accidents happen in the bathroom.

Install a lock box on the front door so caregivers can access the key with a special code and the parent do not need to get up to answer the door.

Talk to your parents and let them know you have hired someone to keep them safe. Let them know how much you worry when you are at work or cannot be there because you have other obligations; and that it will give you peace of mind just knowing someone is there for them.

Is there anything else you'd like to add?

I would like to mention and give kudos to all the wonderful caregivers who work for my home care agency. We hire caregivers who are 50 and older to help our clients who are 50 and older. They have a very special touch with years of experience to share. They can relate better to our clients. Many of our caregivers have been caregivers for their own parents and loved ones. They engage our clients in conversation and activity that keep their minds active and their visits happy. They are not looking at their watches or texting or talking on their cell phones. Their work ethic is impeccable as they arrive on time and stay additional time in the event of an emergency. I am very proud and fortunate to be able to work with such wonderful people, men and women alike.

Lastly, I would like to thank Steve Weiss for being such a wonderful person and mentor and for allowing me the opportunity to be a part of <u>Why We Care</u> because I really do care!

Case Study – Dual In-home Care: Husband Suffers Stroke, Wife Needs Walker

Clients: Terry and James

Scenario:

James suffered a significant stroke limiting him physically. His wife, Terry, is in fairly good health with some pain issues and requires the use of a rollator walker. James experienced long and short-term memory issues leaving Terry as the decision-maker of the household. The couple's medical needs required 24-hour live-in care. The couple had no desire to live in a nursing home or live separately.

Family and Support:

No local family or friends were available for support. Terry and James' distant nephew in Washington were assigned durable power of attorney.

Considerations:

They resided in an independent living cottage in a continued care retirement community with a first-floor set-up. James required a hospital bed and wheelchair. Terry slept in a single bed in the same room. A shower chair and raised toilet seat had been installed.

Lynn: I met Terry and James when they were both patients in a rehabilitation facility. James was admitted into the rehabilitation facility after a stroke. Then Terry fell and was admitted to the same facility for rehab where she shared a room with James. Even though Terry had completed her rehab, she paid privately to stay at the facility until James was discharged home.

A bit of history: The couple had been married at ages 20 and 22. James had been working as a scientist for the U.S. Government and was a veteran of the U.S. Air Force, serving during WWII. Their paths crossed because

Terry worked as a meteorological technician for the National Oceanic and Atmospheric Administration *and* served as a Slavic language translator for the U.S. Government.

James was very quiet and respectful; a complete gentleman in every sense of the word, but Terry ruled the roost! She also loved to sew and had beautiful quilts downstairs in her sewing room. James had taken good care of their finances, and although they did not have family close by to care for them, he had invested in long-term care insurance that eventually paid for their 24-hour live-in care services. This was important because they never wanted to live apart from one another!

Fast-forward: My caregivers began serving Terry and James at their lovely cottage home at the retirement community in February of 2010 when they returned from rehab. James' stroke left him with left-sided weakness and very little use of his left hand. This was quite an emotional and frustrating adjustment for James after losing his self-care capabilities and independent mobility. He could only ambulate short distances with a walker. He was essentially wheelchair bound and could only transfer with assistance. He had a complicated medical history, was prescribed many medications, and saw an oncologist regularly. Later during our care process, he began chemotherapy.

Although Terry's brain function remained sharp, it was appropriate to begin care for both the husband and wife. Terry had significant cardiac history, hearing loss, and was legally blind due to macular degeneration. Due to a back injury and torn rotator cuff, her movement was limited, and she suffered chronic pain.

Both James and Terry were on multiple medications managed by a visiting nurse. Although Terry could get up from a seated position and walk with her rollator walker, she required assistance with showering and grooming and needed help getting out of bed multiple times during the night to use the bathroom. James required assistance with all activities of daily living: showering, grooming, toileting, transferring, medication reminders, and assistance with meals. Our caregivers also shopped for groceries, cooked all meals, cleaned and transported the couple to doctor's appointments.

During the two years, we cared for James and Terry they each had additional hospitalizations with new diagnoses. Shortly after their 65th wedding anniversary, Terry passed away with in-home Hospice care in February of 2012. She fought to live to celebrate "their" day! James survived another nine months in our tender care before he finally left to be with his loving wife.

Our care team is grateful for the opportunity to have been able to care for such a loving couple and keep the two of them together in their own home with dignity, respect, and love.

Case Study – Single Senior with COPD, Helpful Family Nearby

Clients: Carol

Scenario:

Carol lived alone in a two-story house with a stair glide. She had Chronic Obstructive Pulmonary Disease (COPD) and was a regular smoker. She used a walker and required more assistance as she aged.

Family and Support:

Carol's son, Matt, and daughter-in-law, Kerry, called my team to begin in-home services. Matt made himself available as her emergency contact. He was involved in the care process but knew more extensive care was needed.

Considerations:

Carol was a heavy smoker. It was something she enjoyed, so we assigned caregivers who could tolerate the environment. As her health declined, care hours increased from short shifts to 24-hour care.

Lynn: Carol has a wonderful son and daughter-in-law, Matt and Kerry, who introduced our services because he had promised he would let his mother stay in her home. He was a loving son through and through but did not feel entirely comfortable assisting Carol with personal care needs.

When I met Carol, she was alert, but agreed in-home care was appropriate. She knew she needed help with daily living including, bathing, toileting, laundry, cleaning, linen changes, assistance on and off the chair glide, meal preparation and of course, her morning cup of coffee – or two. Carol had been a homemaker and served her country in the U.S. Navy during WWII! Her picture was proudly displayed in the living room of her home! She was a natural beauty! We thank Carol for her service!

We were her companions and friends. She usually sat at her dining room table, enjoying her cigarettes as she worked on a jigsaw puzzle. She was a woman of few words but had a dear heart and was very appreciative of all the assistance we provided. She liked to decorate her house for different holidays, loved Wheel of Fortune and subway sandwiches-they were one of her favorites. They weren't necessarily on her diet plan, but her son approved this once-a-week indulgence. Matt kept his mother's fridge stocked and even transported our caregiver in wintery snow storms! This reminds me of a wintery incident when we couldn't get into the house because a tree had fallen in front of the entrance- you never know when emergency will strike.

Matt was always happy to pick up a care-team member if needed and we loved him for this!

We were initially hired for 2 4-hour shifts 7 days a week; both morning and evening shifts. Our care hours extended gradually over the two-year span we cared for Carol. She eventually needed 24-hour live-in care during her final days under Hospice.

I was proud of my team; on many occasions, my office staffers would actually assist with Carol's shifts and grew to know her family very well. Thanks to our many caring and compassionate caregivers and her loving son, Carol passed in the comfort of her own home just as she wished. We remember Carol with love and affection!

Bio

Lynn Marie Houghton is a registered nurse and the owner and operator of a respected Pennsylvania home care agency which matches persons 50 and older to assist persons 50 and older. Her agency has been serving the Lehigh Valley in Eastern Pennsylvania since 2007, where she initially started her work out of her home.

Lynn's original call for caregiving led her to become a registered nurse in 1989. Her work experience includes working as a staff nurse in a cardiac unit, a visiting nurse for a home care agency, a case manager at a major hospital in Delaware County and another one of the major hospital organizations in the Lehigh Valley as a care manager. Presently she owns and independently operates a home care agency in the Lehigh Valley of Eastern Pennsylvania.

Lynn is very familiar with the in-home needs of seniors because of her nursing experience. In her own words she says, *"The reason I feel so passionate about my work is in loving memory of my grandparents who I was fortunate enough to have until I was 35 years old. Not a lot of people can say that! I believe in my heart they died sooner than they would have or should have because they went to live in a facility against their will (although for the right reasons). I miss them dearly and I want to help other people to find the answer to their loved one's needs in my company- the answers I was unable to find for my own grandparents. This is my tribute to them!"*

Lynn said *"Even as a child, I always had a natural affinity for spending time with my elders and I always wanted to be a nurse. I was even a candy striper at a local hospital at a young age and I thought the idea of opening a home care agency to help seniors stay independent, safe, healthy and happy was my true calling; and so, my journey began…"*

"I want to help seniors stay at home where they really want to be! *We can help people to feel secure and independent instead of helpless and lost! Seniors need to know that they do have a choice about where they live for the rest of their lives."* In her heart, Lynn believes she has and continues to really make a difference in the Lehigh Valley community.

Lynn Marie Houghton, RN, BSN

175 S. 21st Street

Easton, PA 18042

wehelpseniors@ymail.com

Vikki Kalitsi

How long have you been in home health care, and how did you get into it?

Vikki: I started my homecare business in 2001. I got into it by accident. I had just had my first child; she was six months old. I was still at home with her, and my husband was asking, "Are you going back to work?" I said, "No, I'm staying home to raise our child." And he said, "Well, let me find something that you can do from home while you're raising her or some type of home-based business." A couple days later he was at a chamber of commerce meeting and ran into someone who had a home health care franchise. So, after inquiring about the franchise, he came in and he said, "You know, Vikki, I think this is something you can do." I thought: No, not interested; I don't want to have to remotely supervise people. But after deep prayer and I thought, I still was not sure homecare was for me, so I set out to look for part-time work. I had three interviews set up. Before each interview date, each company called back, one by one, to cancel the interview, because they had found someone already. I thought: But they haven't met me! They were like, "No, we'll call you back."

So, I called my old boss, who had been calling me to see if I was coming back. I said, "Well, I think I'll come back part-time," and he said, "You know what... I'm closing the business and moving to South Carolina." And I said, "Okay, Lord, I hear you. Let me go ahead and move forward with this. It's an angel sign." And 16 years later, here I am.

What's your professional background and training?

Vikki: I've always worked in healthcare: healthcare administration, managing physician offices and, urgent care clinics. I've probably worked in every possible discipline that there could be. So, I had a lot of medical knowledge and terminology. I'd seen a lot of the diagnoses that I see today in my work, but I had no idea that it was preparing me for this moment. And ironically, after I left health care after about 15 years I spent a year in advertising, not realizing that that experience also helped me with the home care business.

Home healthcare is such a touching business. What's your passion about it that gets you up day after day?

Vikki: I love helping people. I've always had a heart to serve, and I've always enjoyed being around older people. I think some of that is just based on my own family. My father was 15 years older than my mother. So, in my own home I first saw, the wisdom, the understanding, the guidance, all the positive things, that come with being around older people. They are very grounded.

Tell me about Your company, and the types of clients you help.

Vikki: We are a non-medical home care agency, and we serve individuals who need assistance in their home. It can range from someone who just needs some companion care — which will maybe consist of coming in and helping with some light housekeeping or errands, or assistance to grocery stores — to someone who has cognitive impairment, who cannot do anything on their own and may need total assistance with their hygiene, personal grooming, meal preparation, or medication. We help people who can't go to the bathroom on their own, changing adult diapers. We always say that we are an extension of the family, and we're the alternative to a nurse home or assisted living.

And what's the geographic area that you serve?

Vikki: Prince George's County, Maryland. Prince George's County is in the metropolitan area of Washington, D.C. It's a nice region that we have here, in terms of the demographics in Prince George's County, we have serviced 1000's of patients.

What are the most common obstacles that prevent your clients from being able to stay in their home and get the care they need?

Vikki: Probably the biggest obstacle is money. Home care isn't covered by insurance, and quite honestly, a lot of people don't realize or think that at some point in time they may need this type of service. So, I would say money is the biggest obstacle for many people.

What would your advice be to the reader who's serious about helping a loved one remain at home with care?

Vikki: To really take into consideration what the individuals need are, and to sit down with their loved ones to find out what those needs are. To think about, not just what the need is today, but how it will look five to ten years from now. To talk about other resources out there, like assisted living or nursing homes, if they have to get to that point. Just having a plan, and understanding the person who needs care — what are their desires? To look in the community to see what resources are available.

Do not wait until the time when you need the service. Start educating yourself before you need it, so that when a decision has to be made it can be an educated decision and not one based on emotions. They should check with their local Department of Family Services — some folks call it the Area Agency on Aging. Check with them and see what resources are available. Find out what services their loved ones may be eligible for outside of home care. If they are low income they may be eligible for the Medicaid waiver or some type of assistance from the government. Also, find out through the Department of Social Services what they have to offer.

And to talk to other family members and friends, or church members, who are already on the journey of having to take care of a loved one. To see what they're doing, and not be afraid to talk to people to let them know what you're going through because you always need that support system around you. Many times, we isolate ourselves; we think we're the only ones going through, and many times we're not. If we just let people know what we need, they're able to help us and to provide support.

Are there any pitfalls that the reader should be aware of? What should they be looking for in choosing someone to help them or to help their loved ones?

Vikki: When you're looking for someone to help you, you have agencies like home care agencies that can help. And then some people will look for outside help; you know, someone who's not through an agency, maybe someone recommended to them through a friend. We hear about abuse and financial exploitation, that caregivers may abuse seniors; but a lot of times that's from someone who is not licensed or someone who is not through an agency. They really need to know that they need to do their due diligence when deciding to bring someone into the home. That due diligence is looking to make sure that that person is licensed in the state that they're practicing. Do a national background check with fingerprints on the individual, to see where they've been and if they have committed any crimes outside of your home state. Check their licensing board to see if their license has ever been suspended. Also, talk to family members, and see if they have someone that they can recommend. Check multiple references before bringing someone into your home, and make sure that it's a good fit. A lot of times families are making decisions based on the cost; but sometimes that cost can save you a lot in the long run, by going with an agency where there's due diligence and oversight provided. If something happens to your loved one or something in the home, then the agency is responsible. It's easier to recoup from the agency than it is from an individual. So, do research out there before making that decision to bring someone into the home.

What's the biggest misconception about home health care?

Vikki: The biggest misconception about home healthcare is that someone may come in who may steal from them or may harm their loved one or they may not be able to afford the cost. Many times, when you have abuse, it's usually someone you know: a family member or friend. Many times, it's not someone in the agency. And I think people need to realize that. Also, when you start out with a minimum amount of homecare services it is less expensive than if you need full time around the clock services because your situation has deteriorated. Homecare is less expensive than an assisted living facility and a nursing home. In the home, your care is one to one whereas in a facility you have multiple individuals depending on the service of one individual.

Is there anything the patients and their families can do to prepare for working with you?

Vikki: I always tell family members to think about their expectation of having someone coming into the home. How does that look for you? And what is the goal of having someone come in? Maybe the goal is short-term

— you just need someone to help you regain your strength — or maybe the goal is a long-term goal, because a family member isn't around, and this is a long-term solution for them. They really need to think about their finances, and how long, realistically, they can keep someone in the home; If other family members will be involved in the care and set parameters and expectations for everyone involved in caring for their loved one.

Is there anything else you want to add?

Vikki: We really look at the whole person. We're not just looking at what's going on today; we're looking at, who was this person yesterday before they became frail or infirmed? We take it from a holistic standpoint. We always want to know what's going on with family dynamics when we sit down at the table. Who lives in the home, who is our point of contact and what are the expectations of having someone come into the home.

I cannot just stand by and see someone without any support. Even if you have support like I mentioned earlier, when we look at the individual, we know that there are some clients who need more from us than others. Those who need more from us, we give them more. because if we can make a difference in their quality of life that's payback enough for us.

You have to have a heart to serve. If you're just doing it for the money, get out of the business. You have to make sure you're doing it for the right reasons.

Be transparent. It's like going to the doctor's: if you don't tell them what's wrong, they can't help you. So, for us, if you can't tell me everything that's wrong, and be transparent about the assistance and all the support that you need, then your expectations will not be met. So, in being open to having someone come in, be open to just kind of putting it out there so that they can get what they need.

Case Study – The mortician and his wife with dementia

Client: Louis and Teresa

Scenario:

An 85-year-old mortician, Louis, was admitted to a nursing home after treatment for a pancreatic tumor. He recovered and returned to work, but his wife, Teresa, has dementia and needs ongoing care.

Family and Support:

Louis and Teresa do not have children. Their nephew, Todd, is retired and lives nearby. He helps with appointments and errands. He saw the need for his uncle and aunt to start home care services.

Considerations:

Initially, the situation required only short-term assistance, but eventually expanded to long-term care. Louis is independent; he only needs assistance with medication reminders and household chores. Overall, he is able to make decisions for the household. Teresa's dementia requires her to receive 24/7 care.

Vikki: I met the couple while they were living in a nursing home. Louis was Teresa's primary caregiver, but he became ill and needed rehabilitation. Teresa had dementia, so he also had his wife admitted to the nursing home during his rehabilitation.

When their nephew, Todd, brought me into the nursing home, I approximated one month's care would be needed in order to have Louis safely live back home.

He had been admitted to the nursing home for weight loss and weakness. While he was rehabilitating, we found he had a pancreatic tumor.

Once Louis and Teresa were released, we agreed to provide services for a month, so Louis could have backup support. Louis wished to return to work — he was a mortician and wanted to get back to his regular business operations. He also wanted someone to be at the house to care for his wife while he was gone. My team has been involved for about six months now and will continue for the foreseeable future. This case was initially a temporary home-care situation, turned long-term.

Louis continues to be very independent and in control of our aides' expectations. He enjoys freshly cooked meals daily; southern cuisine is his absolute favorite. After he eats breakfast in the morning, he drives himself to work. Although he doesn't have the strength to perform the burial preparation, he still oversees the administrative function of the business. Teresa and Louis have a dog, Casey, who keeps them company and receives special treatment. While the couple was living in the nursing home, they had a live-in pet sitter take care of Casey back at the house.

Case Study – Individual with M.S.

Client: Jerry

Scenario:

Jerry is 62 years old, has Multiple Sclerosis, and lives alone. He relies entirely on his caregiver for meals, toileting, household needs, and accessing medical treatments.

Family and Support:

One family member had been involved in care, but was financially exploiting him and was prohibited from coming back. Jerry's neighbors check in on him.

Considerations:

The financial exploitation caused trust issues that our home care agency needed to help Jerry overcome.

Vikki: Jerry has M.S., lives alone and is very dependent on our caregivers. He's someone who we would consider a level-three-care patient. He's incontinent and must have meals prepared or brought to him. He has some speech difficulty and relies totally on his caregiver for his daily routines.

He does have friends and neighbors nearby who check up on him and socialize with him daily. He typically eats his breakfast and lunch from home but prefers ordering dinner from local restaurants. He used to work as a school board administrator in another state, so those friends always call to check up on him. Jerry was never married but does enjoy the ladies.

Bio

Vikki Kalitsi is an owner of a Senior Homecare Agency located in Prince George's County Maryland. Her agency has been providing assistance to families and individuals in need of non-medical care since 2001. Ms. Kalitsi deals with families confronted with issues associated with caring their loved ones while raising families and maintaining full-time jobs or they can be dealing with their own aging issues. In these challenging situations, family members can become overwhelmed with the need for assistance in adjusting to their new normal. Ms. Kalitsi assists families by assessing their needs and matching the right caregiver for their loved ones. Ms. Kalitsi also provides information on resources that are available to family caregivers through local, state and national organizations. She educates clients on the importance of taking care of their own help and shows clients how to be proactive with the care for their loved ones, so they are prepared to make the right decisions for a loved one with a chronic illness. Ms. Kalitsi advises individuals to educate themselves on the resources they may need when caring for a loved one. She uses the cradle to grave approach by having them understand that home care may be the first stop in the services that are needed and there may be other services that they will need in between from assisted living communities, nursing homes, and hospice. There needs to be an open and frank conversation about how your loved one may want to live out their final days and have the discussion about what medical interventions they may or may not want while they are still able to be included in the conversation. Having this talk while their loved one is able to make these decisions with the family involved, allows the family to take the guesswork out of "what you would have wanted." Ms. Kalitsi is a founder of the Prince George's Senior Provider Network, serves on the Board of Directors for Maryland Gerontology Association and is a support group leader for the Alzheimer's Association of the National Capital Area.

Vikki Kalitsi, President

Senior Care Angels

301-583-8820

Kunu Kaushal, CSA

Kunu, how long have you been in home health care and how did you get into it?

Kunu: I've been in home health care for about 10 years. My father is a physician, and he has been focused on geriatric care for almost his entire career, and my mother is a critical care nurse by training, and for most of her career has been an administrator for an assisted living facility. Geriatrics was kind of a comfort zone for me. It was an area where I wanted to get deeply involved and have an impact; especially on the non-medical home care side where the need was greater and there was such variance, I think, in quality and the level of services that were being provided.

Family is at the core of everything for us. My grandparents were actually client number one and client number two of the agency. To set the stage and tell you, historically, how this happened... I was born in India and moved here to the States at the age of six. Our family was somewhat split: we had some family in India, and we had some family here in the US. As I grew up in Tennessee it was always deep-seated for me that I was creating a family as I went, and setting in roots. As my grandparents were coming up in age they started to get chronic conditions — their mobility was threatened, medications were a problem, and diabetes became a challenge for them — so they started to spend more time here in the US than in India. It went to six months here, six months there. As you can imagine, they needed a travel companion. I was the oldest grandchild, so I would always take them on the airplane, get them there, and then after a few days get back on the airplane and come back... both ways. So, I had a great affinity with them. I felt very close to them and started to help them with their needs as they were increasing.

During this time, I'd graduated college and had gotten into the medical field as far as medical management, pre-operative and post-operative care, managing nurses and coordinating physicians. One of the things that struck me was I had a great understanding of or affinity to geriatrics. I decided to take on home health and hospice sales. After college, and after working in a hospital system for a while, I then joined a business development team in home health and hospice. I did that for a while and was very successful.

Then I got recruited away to a national consulting agency and was helping other agencies and other individuals understand home health and hospice, and how to sell it and manage it and do a better job.

Quickly after that, I got recruited away to a private duty nursing company. So here I was, mid-twenties, being the administrator over a 20-million-dollar business that did private duty nursing and took care of little children, sometimes just less than a year old, all the way to our oldest client, who was 103 years old. We were providing vent care and trach care, very high skilled clinical needs, in their homes. That agency was in Tennessee as a statewide provider — we had well over three, four hundred employees at the time — and it was an exciting time. But successful agencies get bought and sold, and it was sold.

I had an opportunity either to go on with that company or take what I call "the entrepreneurial leap." What made me decide, very quickly, was the fact that my grandmother and grandfather both were needing more and more care. They were using a home care agency here locally, and I will say that they were receiving subpar levels of care. Now, you should remember: I was coming from working in the clinical model.

I saw nurses, I saw LPN's, and they were doing fantastic levels of care because of our guidance and management skills. We were producing great results in these very complex situations. So, my mind is boggled. Why, when my grandparents are needing no clinical care, but just a caregiver to come in and help with what we call activities of daily living, why was it so hit or miss on quality? Missed visits, caregivers are in and out, background checks aren't being run, quality is bad. And during all this, my grandparents' health is failing more and more. I took the entrepreneurial leap and said: You know what? I'm going to fix the problem in the local market — which I thought was isolated at the time — and I'm going to provide a better level of service. And if nothing else, I will be helping my grandmother and grandfather.

So that is the genesis of our business. We filled a need, and the need was for high-quality home care, and specifically, it was for a family member. And since then, over the last seven years of having my own agency, growing it, and building it, we've gone from client number one and two to over 500 clients on census; which is an incredible blessing.

Home health care is such a touching business. What's your passion about it that gets you up each and every day?

Kunu: There's the compassion in it when you say to yourself: "Gosh, that's just like my family member." My grandmother and grandfather were on services, and it was an incredible honor to give them services through the end of their life. We gave them a sense of independence and choice and dignity, and the ability to be home where they wanted to be. It gave them some level of empowerment that they could choose the type of services they wanted when they wanted them. They weren't doing whatever a facility deemed when they mandate: this is what time breakfast is, and this is the day and time you get a bath.

Through our services I truly feel like they got enjoyment, and, I think it extended their life. Part of it is because, emotionally, when people are feeling like life is worth living they go longer, right? Also, physically, we're making sure their medications are met, their nutritional needs are met, they are in a safe environment, a clean environment, and it's positive. That is part of the reason that our company motto is "Adding years to life and life to years." In clinical institutions you can hook them up to machines, you can pump them full of pharmaceuticals, and you can get the body to live longer. But the second part for us was very key, which is "adding life to years," giving them enjoyment. Nobody's going to be happy when their body's failing, their knees hurt, they can't do the things they want to... But it doesn't have to stop life. And that is why we believe adding life to years is a major component.

That's really it, the reason I get up. Even now I see my grandparents in the names on our client list. When I hear about case conferences, and we're talking about Mrs. Smith or Mr. Jones, it could've easily been Grandma Kaushal or Grandpa Kaushal. For us, knowing that we're creating a difference in these people's lives and truly adding years to life and life to years, it's an incredible feeling that gets you jazzed up, out of bed, and into the office. I have this immense pride when it comes to the fact that every day we can know that we touched so many lives in such an important stage of their life.

Tell me about Senior Solutions Home Care and the types of clients you help.

Kunu: For us, it is the elderly population that needs our assistance and help. Hence, the name became "Senior" and then "Solutions," because we're a solutions provider. It's really interesting the nomenclature that we use, from a national marketing perspective. Some people say," No, No, you've narrowed yourself into the senior market; and what about all these other people you could help?" And I always say, "We want to be very good at servicing people in a very specific demographic." We have clients who aren't seniors, but our target is an elderly individual who wants to remain independent, wherever they might be.

We don't get involved in the clinical side of health care. Simply put, anything that deals with the inside of the body is considered clinical. If we are doing wound management, dealing with bones inside the body, or joint care, those are things that a therapist really needs to get involved in. If you think of the physical body of an individual, we deal with everything on the outside of the body. For example, if it has to do with the activities of daily living — whether it be bathing, toileting, transferring out of bed, housekeeping in their home, meal preparation, running errands — those are the types of activities we're doing. If you think of our typical client, about 95 percent of their needs are on the outside of their body.

One of the beauties of home care is that we can help them as little or as much as they need. We have clients who are very wealthy individuals that have the ability to ask, not "Can I afford this?" but "How much of it do I want?" And then most individuals we have are in the middle, where they say, "Well, this is a part of life, this is an expense I'm going to incur, but it is going to be a means to an end. I have spent my life paying off this home and I want to stay in this home, so let's figure out a way to make this work."

What makes us somewhat unique in the industry is that we also service the other end, which is, they can't afford it. We are a Medicaid provider, which allows us to provide services to individuals who have no funding. These are individuals in very rough situations sometimes, but they are still people. In our business we work with the state, we work with the federal government, and we work with the Veteran's Administration to get them any level of services we can. I try to be very clear in the fact that we will go to whatever ends; if you are an elderly person that needs help, we will get you the care. So, the type of client that we help is quite literally anyone that needs it.

What's the geographic area that you serve?

Kunu: We cover the entire state of Tennessee, all 95 counties within the state. We have eight physical offices throughout the state that becomes essentially like our regional offices. Seven years ago, it was one office — it was one room, actually — so who knows where the future goes for us? Over the next few years, we would love to see ourselves as a regional player within the Southeastern states and serve thousands of more clients.

What are the most common obstacles that prevent your clients from being able to stay in their home and get the care they need?

Kunu: One of the first areas of their life that are threatened through the process of aging is their ability to drive, and so their independence is threatened. In the United States, depending on what part of the country you're from if you don't have the ability to drive you're almost cut off from society. Very rarely are we in metropolitan areas in which you can catch a bus or a subway train. We have a lot of folks that become stuck at home; what, in the medical world or in the health care field, we call homebound. They can't get out to go get groceries or go to the pharmacy to get medications, or to get regular medical appointments with their physician.

Socially, they may have attended church and now they're no longer able to go do that or attend social functions, friends, birthdays, etc. So, this individual is not only in terminology homebound, but they're just plain stuck.

That typically then precipitates other problems. So, soon after they become homebound they start having nutritional issues, they're not eating quite as well as they should. They have pharmaceutical issues where they're not taking their medications as they should. And at other times they've gotten new chronic illnesses that are going undiagnosed because they haven't gone to a doctor recently. So now their ability to get proper care is becoming impacted.

Then the next obstacle that comes in is personal care, as their health continues to degrade. For example, it's harder to get in and out of the tub, so now we've got a physical barrier and maybe hygiene is being impacted. It is difficult to get on and off the toilet. We're having difficulty cooking in the kitchen because we can't stand up, or don't feel comfortable standing for lengthy periods of time or reaching for dishes in the top cabinet. And because we don't feel comfortable cooking, we start going to frozen meals and microwaving meals which are chock full of salt. Very quickly we've got an individual whose weight is out of control, up or down, whose salt intake is out of control, up or down, and nutritionally they're becoming sicker and sicker.

I don't like to start with personal care because people don't see the signs right away, but the eventuality of it is now suddenly, we need help with bathing and toileting and dressing and oral hygiene; some of these almost institutional-type services that you would see in a nursing home.

But the main true obstacle is denial. Through this whole path that I just told you about there were moments in which someone, whether it be the client or the family, had the thought: maybe we should get some help, maybe we should do something different, but we were in denial. As a nation, and as a people… just as a human race, actually… no one wants to talk about the aging process.

We will have clients that are well into the late stages of this path, and they're at a point where they can't drive, they don't have the proper medicines, they're not eating well, they don't feel comfortable bathing. And I have told someone, "You need help and we can help you, or get you help, but you are going to have to do something," and had them look at me and say, "Oh, I'm fine, I don't need it." So, denial is certainly the number one obstacle of all of those.

What is your advice to the reader who's serious about helping a loved one remain at home with care?

Kunu: The number one thing I would tell you is: call an expert, or at least someone that is involved in this type of care in your community. A home care company can be a great resource, but the number one reason you probably don't call a home care agency is you feel like they are going to try to "sell you something." I think a good, high-quality provider is not going to do that. They're going to try to steer you in the right way. As a company, if we ever do what we call a "free in-home consultation," we truly talk about options. A good home care agency should be able to tell you what options there are and what you have.

I always present three options; it's one of our company's standards that we use. One is to do nothing; and we will tell you, if you do nothing, these are the things that could or would happen. You may not need to do anything; maybe we're having a bad blip in time and things aren't so good right now, but it's fixable.

The second option is to get help through home care. Aging in place becomes a situation where home care, home health, DME, and other types of resources in the community can get involved and can help a person stay. The third option is the one that everyone wants to avoid, but it may be appropriate: you may need to relocate into a community, into a facility. Maybe you're just too far along in the aging process or needs, and it's very risky for you to not do that unless you've got the financial means to bring in all the potential care you would need.

Another resource is a senior center. Almost every senior center in every community has resources available to them as a point of contact. They are more than just an activity center; they are chock full of experts and contacts and individuals that can help with anything from transportation to connecting you with home care or connecting you with geriatric care management.

The internet is chock full of information. Most elderly folks typically have one or more chronic disease processes. It doesn't take much to get on the internet, look at YouTube for videos, go to a library… wherever. But the Internet's the best and easiest way. Search out all the information you can on that disease process.

So, let me give you an example. My grandmother had COPD, which is Chronic Obstructive Pulmonary Disease. The first thing we did was we got online and learned everything about COPD. It is much deeper than the brochure you get at the doctor's office. That's good initial information, but online there are videos and you hear stories and make connections, and there are resources and support groups that are available. By studying it you get a true picture of what you can expect in the future and what you currently should really be worried about. We very quickly found out that oxygen was going to become a big issue, so we needed to go ahead and start talking to DME companies, durable medical equipment: what type of oxygen options would we have in the home? Then we also found out that exerting herself would get her to a point where her blood oxygen levels would get too low.

Although she really enjoyed it — my grandmother was very prideful in her home — however, her health was at a point that she didn't need to be doing housekeeping and chores. So that was one of the first few tasks that we took away from her… she could still direct it, she could still help in certain ways, but the majority burden of that task we took away. It had nothing to do with her doctor and it had nothing to do with her health care provider; we just knew that this was going to cause a serious issue over time.

Now, keep in mind we had a leg up and a head start with our family, having a health care background. But whenever someone calls us and asks for services, we respond to them by email with two to three links to online resources, so they can educate themselves. Knowledge is truly powerful. When you're talking to a home care company, you should know more than the home care provider that is going to provide these services. It puts you in a position of empowerment. You will see a quality provider stand out, whether it be a physician, durable medical equipment provider, or a community if you're going to relocate. But especially in-home care, you are going to be able to tell the difference between a good provider, a lackluster provider, and a poor provider. You know what to expect, you know what's going to be important and how to build the care and expectations you want.

Would you say there are any pitfalls that the readers should be aware of, like what should they look for in choosing someone to help them?

Kunu: There are two categories of pitfalls that are worth mentioning. One is what I call operational, and the other applies to the caregivers, the service delivery person.

So, operational. There are many franchise agencies in the nation today that are very cookie cutter, copy-and-pasting their model across the country. I'm not going to get into whether it's good or bad, but the point is that they all have operating methods that they use. We are an independent agency, and one of the things that makes us very nimble is that we change our operations based on what we're finding out every day.

Let's say you need to call someone and talk to them after hours. The biggest problem you will have, typically, is getting in touch with someone after hours. That is, I believe, where an agency shows their true professionalism or not, and their ability to handle a problem. Home care is a 24/7 business. 24/7 does not care about weather, holidays, calendar date, or if it's a special Sunday or not; your loved one is going to need that help and support. I would look at a home care agency that can meet that standard operationally. What if you need something at eight o'clock at night? What if mom calls at ten o'clock at night and says, "Oh my gosh, I forgot I've got a doctor's appointment tomorrow." How will the company help to accommodate or meet needs that are very quickly changing? What happens if there's a complaint, or if you have an issue? What if we don't like our caregiver? Go ahead and ask those questions. How that agency answers will give you a true sense of how capable and willing it is to be professional.

Do not judge a company by a brochure, but certainly realize that it's a good litmus test, at least in the beginning. If a company has a poor standard in their presentation, they'll probably have a poor standard in their delivery.

The second pitfall that is important is the actual caregivers, the service delivery people. You want to look at some things, like… Do they have a uniform? We at Senior Solutions Home Care are anti-nursing home… And I want to clarify, we're not against nursing homes, but we're anti- the look and feel of it. So, we don't do scrubs, we don't call our clients "patients," and we don't have a nurse that does an assessment. Now, certain states require that; but we try to keep it very much a concierge style of service, regardless of financial ability. It doesn't matter if you're on Medicaid, we're providing you a higher level of service. So, our caregivers wear polo's that are embroidered, with typically khaki pants and solid colored shoes, and they wear a name tag.

One of the things you should always ask is: Can I meet one of your caregivers? I understand that won't be the one, but I'd be curious to meet one and see what services are like. The other question that I would ask is: What does your guarantee of service look like? For example, if a caregiver isn't here at the start of care, what is the backup? What is the plan? A true high-quality agency will tell you plan B, C, and maybe even D of getting you the care that you need.

If you're in a state that has a home care license, educate yourself on the licensing requirements in your state. One of the best clients that we've ever had, in the sense that they were well-informed, had gone online and read the requirements of an agency very quickly — it's about six pages.

They were able to ask me, "Are you licensed?" Yes, we're licensed. And they say, "Well, do you check for felonies for seven years?" Yes, we do. "Do you do drug testing on all your caregivers?" Yes, we do. What I understood very quickly is this person's not only very well informed, but they're going to ask all the other agencies these same questions. And they'll quickly find there are agencies that don't even follow their own standards in their state.

They asked us about 20 questions and we could answer those, all in a positive manner, and then we were able to tell them about 40 other things that we do that are above and beyond the standard.

What do you think are the biggest misconceptions about home health care?

Kunu: The biggest misconception is that it's free. There's a generation that we're servicing that was told that Medicare would be the solution to all their problems in the future, kind of the golden ticket for health care as they got older. And Medicare is a strong foundation for medical services; the issue is that aging isn't always a medical problem. So, by the analogy I used earlier — we in our company provide non-medical home care, we deal with everything on the outside of the body — Medicare deals with basically everything on the inside of your body. So, they pay for the hospital, they pay for the ambulance, the rehab, they pay for the home health. In that way, Medicare becomes a standard, and I think a lot of our clients, or their adult children that are looking for services, think that we are also the same thing.

Unfortunately, home care does have a cost. Here's an important point, however, to put out: the average cost of assisted living care in the United States is 48,000 dollars a year. The average cost of nursing home care in the United States is closer to 77,000 dollars a year for a private room and slightly less for a shared room. Nationally, the typical expense that a home care client spends is about 18,000 dollars a year — there are people who are spending quite a bit more and there are people who are spending quite a bit less, but on average it comes out to about $18,000.

One thing that we always try to clarify for folks is that we are, at the end of the day, the best financial option for an individual, and probably the best-case scenario in the long run.

So, let me give you an example. Let's say you have an individual and you're thinking about financial planning, and you say: We're just going to go ahead and bite the bullet and move to assisted living; we're going to spend about 48,000 dollars a year for the next five years, on average. That lasts for about five years, and then all of a sudden, we get into nursing home placement for an additional three to four years, at... let's call it 70,000 dollars.

Using home care, a person could have spent 18,000 dollars a year for the next seven years or ten years, whatever it might be, making those higher-cost alternatives truly an alternative of last resort. It would be the equivalent of saying, "Gosh, I really need a new car," and then immediately going in and buying a brand-new Ferrari. Yes, for some people it makes sense, but others just need to know what other options are available to them.

The biggest misconception would be around the cost of home care: that it might be free; and then what the true impact of cost is because everything else is much more expensive.

Is there anything else that patients and their families can do to prepare for working with you?

Kunu: Have a conversation with each other. What's most important to us? Finances will always be a factor, and we always talk about that. But there are other components to this. Always come at it with the perspective of: what would you like to do over the next five years? If your health gets worse, how do you see things going?

We find that there are certain clients that are very open and receptive to care, and they say, "Oh my goodness, I'm so glad you're here, I can't wait to get started because I've needed this for quite some time." But we have other clients who say, "I don't need help." In those scenarios, we become a personal assistant, or we become a housekeeper that also helps to give you a bath every now and again.

It's all about approach, and having that conversation is a very positive thing. We have sometimes facilitated those conversations, and that is something that, as an agency, we're happy to do. We set up a meeting, we come in as an outside expert, and we start to ask some of those questions.

But certainly, the best thing you can do to prepare is have a frank conversation. Talk about it openly, and make sure that we are giving individuals the dignity that they deserve to have, some level of empowerment in how they spend their golden years.

Anything else you want to add?

Kunu: The one thing that I would add is that I'm very interested that we, maybe as a society, start to really focus on long-term care. I don't mean in the form of a facility or a business or even home care. As we look at different cultures around the world, there are very tight family units; and here in the United States, we covet our independence.

It's my hope for us as a society that we honor our elders. That we start to involve them more in our community and try to give them more chances for access, to be able to get places.

There are two areas in our business that are going to that end. We are going to focus on care management more because we hope to be able to give guidance and advice to folks and families earlier on in the process. And the second thing, which is a recent project for me, is to start looking at transportation. Our hope is we can catch folks even earlier on and give them the independence they deserve.

Case Study: Husband with Alzheimer's, cognitively sharp wife with mobility issues

Client: Janet and Cliff

Scenario:

The couple lives in a senior community in an independent townhouse. The couple is in their early 70's. The husband has Alzheimer's and dementia (what we call "sundowners," referencing the daily progression of the illness by nightfall). Janet had mobility issues and was heavily dependent on her walker. She was the mind and he was the body: Janet would have to speak directions to Cliff in order to execute tasks around the home.

Family and Support:

The couple was of average financial bearing. One daughter, Jessica, lived farther away, while the other daughter, Coleen, lived close by; both of whom were estranged from each other. Jessica wanted her parents to move in with her in the Northeast and Coleen wanted them to stay put and have her take financial control of the couple's assets. Between dementia, physical ailments, and conflicting family interests, the situation called for outside assistance.

Considerations:

Cliff and Janet wanted to stay together, which initially precluded them from choosing a memory care facility for Cliff's ailments. Janet wanted independence and control of her financial and living decisions, so my company made sure she felt empowered. The home needed some retrofit in the bathroom for safety. Cliff is a veteran, so they wanted to utilize their veteran benefit in some capacity.

Kunu: When we met Janet, she was in denial of her own physical abilities and because she was still "getting things done," she wasn't worried. Our biggest challenge was Cliff who suffered from Alzheimer's and dementia. There was an extreme risk of him wandering throughout the night. He could quite easily open the door and just take off walking, while Janet wouldn't be able to keep up. The bathroom was not fitted for someone of her needs and the kitchen was too tight for her and a walker or wheelchair.

Janet initially enlisted our care because she felt her daughters were maybe trying to take control of her money. Jessica, in favor of having her parents to move in with her, planned on charging her mother rent. Daughter Coleen wanted to take over the finances because she wanted to make sure the money was being spent well. The irony of the entire situation is Janet would overspend on QVC, Amazon, and the Home Shopping Network — no exaggeration, she had at least four or five packages show up every single day— just to show her daughters that her money was her money.

Cliff was one of the happiest individuals I've ever met. He was blissfully ignorant to the drama, and that's one of the unfortunate, but fortunate aspects of Alzheimer's or dementia. As long as there was a smiling face and people around, he was okay and engaged during the daytime. His body was perfectly fine, but he was trapped in the house because his wife was homebound. He so desperately wanted to get out, stretch his legs and go do something, but he couldn't be trusted to do so safely.

For this scenario, we started very small. We provided services two to three days a week; we got them in contact with a home health service to help Janet her physical ailments to begin improving her mobility. We also hired someone to retrofit their bathroom and install one strategically placed grab bar. For mobility around the kitchen, we were able to find her a slimmed-down wheelchair that would fit its dimensions. We were also able to give her some sense of independence by taking Cliff out on trips a few times a week. We would walk in the mall or go to a park that he enjoyed which allowed him to get some of his energy out. Now by the end of the day, Cliff no longer felt like he wasted the day doing nothing.

As health issues progressed, we kept adding more and more service hours to a point where it became too expensive. Standing at a crossroads, we took all their finances into account and made the recommendation that now would an appropriate time to move into a community. We were able to find them a community with a memory care unit and an assisted living community that was joined, so they could spend their days together.

Unfortunately, they had to sleep in separate rooms, but they were already accustomed to that setup, so they were willing to compromise. We were able to find them funding from the Veteran's Administration who picked up at least 20 to 30 percent of the cost of care.

We gladly welcomed the two daughters during case conferences and communication, and telephone calls, so they felt involved in the care as it proceeded. We serviced Janet and Cliff for over three years in total. Last, we know, they continue to be healthy and happy.

Case Study - Individual who lives alone

Client: Paul

Scenario:

Paul was at risk of falling. He was in his mid-80's, six feet four and 200 pounds, living in a nursing home. He was unhappy with the care and would often make a scene inside the facility. Paul was a career pharmacist, so standards of care, his medication and routines were very important to him. He was very detail-oriented individual and was very unhappy having a different caregiver every day. He needed one-on-one care.

Family/Support:

Paul had a niece who lived relatively close by, but she had no clinical or medical instincts and didn't know how to care for him. They were far apart enough in their relationship where they needed outside help. Paul had church friends who would check up on him.

Considerations:

Paul wanted independence, reliability, and customize care tailored exactly to his preference. He wanted to spend his last moments, no matter how soon or long they would be, at home and nowhere else.

Kunu: Paul was at risk for falls, so he was living in a nursing home. He was so unhappy in the facility that he would make a scene almost every day because he wanted to go home. It's amazing to say, but in your mid-80's, when most people who need home care don't have their faculties, Paul's main issue was that he couldn't stand for long periods of time.

He had a niece and a nephew that lived in the same town, and they would help with things like groceries, running errands, and going to the pharmacy. They were happy doing so for some time until his personal care needs escalated; this was too far outside of their comfort zone. He also had visitors that would come in from church and kind of check in on him, bringing him a casserole that might last two or three days. That was the extent of his circle of care.

The biggest obstacle was how Paul wanted a lot of care, but wasn't quite prepared for what it would cost. For many years he had never been involved in his financial dealings; he had some sort of trust that maintained his finances. I personally handled the in-home consult for him, walked him through everything, had the conversation with the family, etc. We were doing well until we started talking about the cost of care. I was a little stunned because when I told him what it was costing him to stay in the community versus what it would cost to be home, he immediately said yes, let's do homecare right away. When he found out we were the lower-cost alternative, he signed up for 24/7 one-on-one care and was very happy.

There was a ton of clutter in Paul's house - rooms, bedrooms, hallways, and the kitchen was just full of a lot of things. We made it one of our care goals to reduce the clutter not only for our client (so that he could feel secure in his space) but for the safety of our caregivers. In a matter of weeks, with his help and his guidance, we moved things into the garage or out to the dump. He felt like he was involved in the process instead of somebody else doing all the work. We were able to turn an obstacle into a project.

Paul probably could have endured the nursing home for a couple of years, but stayed on as our client for five years. We had a very consistent staff over those five years; he had some caretakers come and go, but the majority were people he liked. He was very happy to have been able to maintain his daily routine, and truly had his wish of spending his last moments in his home come true. We were blessed to be able to service him and have an impact on his life for five years, which is astounding — the average home care client is with us about 14-24 months. So, it was a great result for both of us.

Bio

Kunu Kaushal is one of the latest influencers in the long-term care/ health care space in Tennessee. He studied business management at the University of Alabama at Birmingham and proceeded to work in multiple health care fields focused on the highest quality of care.

Passionate about impacting the health care space, founding a senior care agency was a natural fit. With the motivation of helping his own grandparents as his first clients, Kunu started Senior Solutions Home Care in 2010. Today the company services the entire state out of multiple offices. In his free time, Kunu enjoys family time with his wife Jill and their three daughters. As an eternal scholar, you'll often find Kunu researching or learning more about the art of entrepreneurship. Grateful for the hundreds of families that trust the care of their loved ones to his team, Kunu focuses on being the market leader in the industry.

Kunu Kaushal, CSA

Founder & CEO - Senior Solutions Home Care

http://seniorsolutionshomecare.com/

615-377-6566

kunu@notcanoe.com

Judy Loubier, PT, CSA, CDP

How long have you been in home health care and how did you get into it?

Judy: As far as my team is concerned, we have been in home health care for just about four and a half years now. In August 2012, we became licensed in New Hampshire as a home care service provider agency. We also met with a national home health care franchise beginning in March of 2012.

My personal reasons for breaking into the home health care industry began with the story of my parents and a touch of serendipity. Originally New York residents, my mother, and father moved to sunny Florida and had lived there for over 20 years. They very much enjoyed staying active, playing golf three to four times a week. In January 2012, my mother's doctor thought she might have lung cancer, so she underwent surgery to remove two lobes from her right lung.

My two sisters and I would take turns flying down to visit, staying for five days at a clip during the first three weeks of her recovery. Her recovery was going seemingly well when suddenly, four days after the last sister in the rotation returned home, my mother suffered a stroke. She was in dire condition and was immediately placed in an acute care hospital. She spent three months in rehab after another procedure. My two sisters and I quickly began planning more flights to Florida.

My parents held very traditional roles. After my mother's stroke, he had trouble managing the household and life in general. My father's mantra was, "In sickness and in health." He was with my mother all day long and never left her bedside for three whole months. It was very hard to get him to do anything for himself but sit by her bed.

My sisters and I started taking turns flying down to make sure my mother's rehab was managed properly. During one of my visits in March of 2012, I was trying to work out some kinks in the rehabilitation protocol. While I was there, my mother had a transient ischemic attack and was moved back to the acute care hospital.

I had an obligation to fly back to New Hampshire the next day because I managed an outpatient rehab department at the time and we were putting on a large community event that had been planned months in advance. I also had to rush home for my son's first high school state wrestling tournament; as a mom, you want to be there for your child's special moments. I had so many responsibilities buzzing in my mind, and my mother was still in the acute care hospital by the time I reached the airport.

As I waited to board the plane, I let myself pray. It was a very firm prayer, probably the most fervent prayer of my life up until that point. I said over and over, "God, how do you want me to help my parents? How can I help my parents?" I boarded the plane, sat down in my seat, and I took out the United Airlines magazine. The first page I turned to displayed an ad for senior care. I had read this magazine on the flight down to Florida but never saw the ad before. This sign jumped out at me: God was answering my prayer.

The bottom of the ad read, "Franchise opportunities available." I wrote down all the information

My husband picked me up when I landed. I showed him the ad information and told him, "This is what I need to do with the rest of my career."

In many ways, it felt like it was God answering two prayers: my prayer for my parents' health, and my prayer regarding my career path. Although I loved my job, I'd been a physical therapist for a little more than 25 years at that point, and my back was starting to feel the strain. I specialized in young children with severe disabilities, particularly children with nonverbal and severe motor disability cerebral palsy, so I was doing a lot of lifting. I had been in prayer for a couple of years asking guidance as to what I should do regarding my career because I knew my back wouldn't hold up for another 10 or 15 years.

I called and set up an interview with the senior care franchise. I wanted to have a discussion with them to better understand their drive, ambition, and passion. They also needed to learn if we had the great amount of "heart" they look for in a senior care franchise owner. Next thing you know, we took three trips to Pennsylvania and purchased the franchise. We were the first and only of its kind in New Hampshire.

You mentioned you were a physical therapist. Could you tell me about your professional background and training?

Judy: I always knew I wanted to be a physical therapist, but the urge probably started when my cousin was born.

My mother always had a special place in her heart for children and vulnerable people and I took after her. My sisters and I would spend time volunteering in the hospital and teaching Sunday school.

When I was 10 or 12 years old, my cousin was born with Down syndrome. I casually recall my mother telling me something to the effect of, "Don't worry, a physical therapist will work with her and teach her how to walk." I remember thinking: "Wow that sounds perfect for me."

I attended Northeastern University in 1980, majoring in physical therapy. I graduated in 1985 with a Bachelor's degree in physical therapy and worked primarily with children with severe disabilities.

I also spent time working with the elderly throughout my career; some in-home care, some in assisted living, and some in skilled nursing facilities. I served them for the same reason I began working with children. Seniors are a bit vulnerable and really need somebody to understand them on a deep level in order to provide the right care. This line of work spoke to me. So, it was the people on either end of the age spectrum that I connected with most in my years as a physical therapist.

Home health care is a touching business. What's your passion about it that gets you up day after day?

Judy: My passion is the blessing of getting to know the people we help. We have an opportunity to bless people: not just by providing the services they need, but by creating a relationship and getting to know them as unique individuals.

We've been able to assist a gentleman who was a naval commander on a warship during World War II. He was a difficult man to provide service for because everything in his home had to operate with precision. It seems that might have been how he kept people alive in World War II; he needed everything to be exact. As he aged, he developed dementia. We came to the understanding that he was not being difficult, but that he had made a sacrifice for our country requiring him to be this way. This wasn't hard work, this was an honor.

We've worked with people who were raised in Manchester, our biggest city in New Hampshire. A lot of French-Canadians had moved into Manchester, especially on the west side. It was a blessing to hear their stories about moving from Canada, learning to speak English, and what life was like for them in school. Some of them never traveled further than Manchester but stayed in the town to raise families with unique stories of their own. It's very much been an honor to get to know each person.

What really tugs at my heart is this sense of the elderly being lonesome. I think their biggest fear is being alone. We are present and have an opportunity to engage them on a personal level, and reassure them they don't have to face the day alone. Troublesome tasks and questions are answered like: Who's going to make my lunch? Who will pick up my medications from the pharmacy? To whom do I tell my story?

I think that's what the elderly wants most: somebody who wants to know who they truly are. This is what gets me up day after day.

Tell me about your agency, and the type of clients you help.

Judy: Sure! I'll give you a few examples.

The youngest people we've helped were probably a little under 60 years of age with younger-onset Alzheimer's. These two separate gentlemen I am referring to really needed companionship. Their wives had to make the adjustment as the new breadwinners. We were providing meal preparation and a lot of companionship. We've had some younger clients with younger onset dementia as well.

The oldest client we've assisted is 103. There have been times when families ask our providers to stay in the room with them as their elderly family member witnesses their last moments of life. Our providers become more than a support network; they become a part of a family of care.

We also provide a huge time range of service shifts from three hours once a week to 24/7 home care. We provide services including very active, engaging companionship and cognitive activities, to helping with personal care.

Another patient that comes to mind is a 95-year-old woman who's an incredibly hot ticket. She's very sharp and manages her life beautifully. Unfortunately, she's losing her vision and can no longer drive, but she wants to make sure to get out of her house at least once a week. She and her provider have a great time together, going out to lunch, shopping, and attending scheduled appointments.

In this case, the client told her provider she had seen her doctor who informed her that the vision condition had become terminal. The client's daughter was having trouble handling the news, so the provider came and met with me to discuss some talk strategies for these heavy conversations. I also brought up the need for a Portable Do Not Resuscitate [PDNR] form. A lot of people don't know about the PDNR. The ill person might have a Do Not Resuscitate order on file at the hospital, or even in their estate plan, but an EMT is not permitted to follow those orders. They need to see the bright pink PDNR form. It's recommended the patient hang it on their refrigerator and tear off the two cards toward the bottom, keeping them in a wallet of some sort.

At the next visit to the doctor, the client and her provider mentioned the PDNR. The doctor thought it was a fabulous idea and was grateful the discussion had come up. When the daughter finally heard it explained from the doctor's perspective, she was completely on board. The client called us to communicate how grateful she was about the result and felt she would have neglected to speak to the doctor if it hadn't been for our guidance.

I'm grateful to serve a range of people and have a range of opportunities to be helpful.

What's the geographic area that you serve?

Judy: We can serve all of New Hampshire, a small portion of Massachusetts, and Southern Maine.

How many patients do you work with at a time?

Judy: We have a census of about 80 to 90 clients.

What are the most common obstacles that prevent your clients from being able to stay in their home and get the care they need?

Judy: The most common obstacles presented to us *before* we start care are the client's inability to tend to their own personal care needs in a safe manner. They may fall during dressing, they are at risk in the shower, may forget to shower altogether, or forget to change clothes. They might also need medication reminders and help with meals.

We always try to assess the family and client's wishes once they reach out to us for personal care assistance, meal preparation, medications, and more.

What would be your advice to the reader who is serious about helping a loved one remain at home with care?

Judy: My first piece of advice would be to start early. I think it's important to begin reaching out to home care companies prior to the crisis; before your family member is in the hospital for three days with a urinary tract infection, and a discharge planner is telling you that the doctor will only send them home with 24-hour care. After the crisis, it's often that a family member will be sent home with no planned care. Starting early is a major benefit, even if care shifts take place only two or three times a week where we housekeep, shop for groceries, take the client with us during errands, and oversee personal care. Sometimes the client just wants somebody in the house while they take a shower for safety reassurance or to provide companionship.

It's very natural for a client to comply with a doctor ordering 24/7 care, but it's overwhelming when they have no idea what home care actually entails. It's a stressful to be *reactive* in this scenario. Now families are pressed for time because they have to get back to their own lives and jobs. If you're proactive, you can choose and progress with the care that's right for you. Caregivers that begin service for a client in the early stages can catch health changes relatively early on before a crisis ensues.

Are there any pitfalls the reader should be aware of? What should you look for in choosing someone to help them and their family?

Judy: If I were searching for a caregiver for my parents, I would look for a good listener. I think it's important for the caregiver to understand the client as an individual and sympathize with the stress the adult children or spouse is going through. Although the 8-10 years of experience might ring true, the attitude of a caretaker who enters a situation as if they already know exactly what a client needs might inhibit a proper approach. A specific client's needs and desires might go unaddressed if a caretaker doesn't listen! It's important to assign a good listener or someone who might even have personal care experiences within their own family, so they can better relate to and soothe the stress of the client's children.

I would also search for an agency or person who works well on a team. I'd ask myself, what is this agency's relationship with other home health agencies? What is their relationship with hospice companies? …With hospital staff, rehab staff, and skilled nursing facility staff? Agencies working in tandem make for good transitions: a good transition from home to hospital, from hospital to the skilled nursing facility, and then home again.

It's also very important to know when Medicare will give coverage, when they're going to discharge, and when we, as a home care agency, must pick up the coverage after Medicare ends. When to consider hospice care is another huge consideration. The caregiver should ease the burden of that decision and be present for that transition for the family. They should work with a hospice agency closely, to provide a continuum of care.

What's the biggest misconception about home health care?

Judy: To me, "home health care" typically means the medical portion Medicare will cover, versus "home care" meaning the portions Medicare will not cover.

The biggest myth about home health care is that the family thinks it will carry on in perpetuity. It does not. For a client to participate in Medicare, certain criteria and health goals need to be met. If the client hits a plateau, no longer makes gains, or they're going out of the house too often, they will not qualify for home health care. Medicare will insist on discharging at a certain point.

If you're relying on home health care — for example: a nurse, a nurse assistant, a physical therapist, an occupational therapist, maybe even a speech therapist — 1) Your needs won't disappear once Medicare stops coverage and 2) Medicare does not feel the need to fill that gap in the service. They will not go to the mailbox and get your mail; they're not going to help you pay your bills on an ongoing basis; they don't cook meals; they can't go to the pharmacy and pick up your medications, or get your groceries. There's a big gap in service between home health care and the way we actually live our lives.

A lot of times hospitals share in that misconception. Families will say, "Oh no, our services are all set up," because their social worker set up a visiting nurse, a PT, an occupational therapist and maybe a nurse assistant. The availability of those services is based on an evaluation, so those services paid for by Medicare are temporary. The family doesn't realize that the licensed nursing assistant might only be at the client's house once or twice a week even though their sickly mother likes to bathe three times a week.

In terms of home care, like my agency, I think people tend to see it as a light touch. They don't realize that a home care agency can stay with you until the very end of your life. It doesn't have to be a stopgap before the nursing home. It really, truly can be *your* decision to stay home; with home care and home health services, you can stay in your house right through to the end of life.

Is there anything that patients and their families can do to prepare for working with you?

Judy: I would suggest being as open and honest as possible. There's no reason to hide anything. For example, a family might be considering home care for their mother, but they're also visiting assisted living facilities and nursing homes before making a final decision. Sometimes the family keeps the other considerations a secret because they are afraid a home care agency might not provide the coverage they need or prioritize them. For us, that's a complete misconception. We base our services on finding the right match because that relationship is the heart of everything. We want clients to look forward to seeing our providers. If our process is working well and they love each other, we're not changing the service.

If I know a family is considering a different option, I can help them. Maybe that means going on the tour with them. I can help them sort through the differences in the facilities because we're constantly working *with* the facilities. We've even had providers help transition clients to memory care or assisted living because it was too disruptive and difficult for the family to execute. Our providers would visit with clients for a few weeks as they acclimated to their new living arrangement for a smooth transition. It's so much better to be open, honest, and to use me as a resource because this is my passion.

Is there anything else you'd like to add?

Judy: It's really ingrained in our hearts to be sure that people don't feel alone in this journey. In fact, both of my parents passed away this past year. About a year after my mother's stroke, my parents ended up moving from Florida back to New Hampshire to be near me. They had the choice to have me renovate my home, move in, and be alone all day while my husband and I go to work, but they were very social people. For that reason, they decided to live in an assisted living facility 15 minutes away from my home. There were times when I was there for a couple of hours a week and then there were times when I was there nearly every single day, sometimes a couple of times a day. When my dad died in July, I visited my mother every day. At that point, her vascular dementia caused by her stroke required her to be on a memory unit.

As a daughter, you can feel very alone in this process. My agency goes the extra mile so that the adult children don't feel alone. We're a resource they can call anytime. My phone is on all the time; I will answer at 2:00 in the morning if need be. We're there for them. The client is not alone.

I once had a little 88-year-old lady call me at 3:30 in the morning, wondering what her schedule was for the rest of the week. When I saw her later that day she was so apologetic, but I reassured her and said, "That's what I'm here for." I'd rather help her get through her sleepless anxiety than worry about how much I slept that night.

As an elderly person in the home and as an adult child caring for them, it's a long journey that takes many twists and turns. There are times when you just feel so alone. We want to be with people, so they don't feel isolated. That's our mission.

Case Study – Married Couple – Husband has Parkinson's, Wife has Alzheimer's

Client: Frank and Linda

Scenario:

Frank, although cognitively sharp, has Parkinson's and needs assistance bathing, dressing, and preparing meals. His wife, Linda, has Alzheimer's and needs assistance planning and overseeing meals, medication, and overall care. They live in a very old house that presents safety risks.

Family and Support:

The couple's children are very supportive, involved and caring, but all live out-of-state. Their daughter-in-law contacted us to set up care. They do not have local friends who can help.

Considerations:

There is a significant risk of falling, medication errors, and missing meals. Frank needs more personal care than Linda. Caregivers are present every day, from 9:00 a.m. to 8:00 p.m. The house environment and Frank's walker were unsafe, so a physical therapist was brought in to assess and correct the situation. Linda is unaware of how drastically her Alzheimer's inhibits her ability to manage the household successfully, so care providers work alongside her in such a way where her power and ownership is still maintained and respected.

Judy: When Frank and Linda were referred to us, Frank had just come out of rehabilitation. They had been living for eight weeks with one of their sons, Jacob. Jacob's wife Jessica reached out to us because Frank and Linda's children wanted to move back to their home in New Hampshire, a 150-year-old home built by his family.

Some great backstory: Frank went to MIT and worked on rockets for the U.S. Army. Linda taught as a home demonstration agent, teaching homemaking skills in 40 different towns in New Hampshire. Pretty amazing! Frank's Uncle Jim was one of the first engineers of the Flying Yankee, a train that took its first trip from Boston to Maine in 1935. The couple's house sits near the railroad tracks for the Flying Yankee. When Frank was eight years old, Uncle Jim would ride by the house, slow the train, and throw candy to his nephews as it was going by. It's always so exciting to hear the unique stories my clients share.

Although charming, this old New England home is very old and poses some safety risks requiring extra attention.

Frank has Parkinson's Disease, he had a stroke six years ago and cardiac bypass surgery five years ago. Linda has Alzheimer's Disease and is quite mobile. Linda believed she properly oversaw her husband's care needs: dressing him, cooking meals, etc. However, the moment my team entered the home they could see signs of her forgetfulness and confusion; there was a fair amount of clutter, food had been incompletely prepared, and toast left in the toaster from the day before.

Frank's personal care entails bathing, toileting, assistance getting dressed, and shaving. Linda is not fully able to plan meals anymore but participates under the direction of the provider. Our providers help make certain that care is coordinated, fresh food is kept in the refrigerator, and the couple's medication reminders are on schedule.

We are currently providing care 11 to 12 hours a day for Linda and Frank (who recently celebrated his 90th!), while the family still participates on weekends. The family is committed to keeping the couple together and it pays off in emotional dividends. The couple still falls asleep in bed holding hands after talking about their day. It's the sweetest picture. Although Frank's obstacles are many, without our homecare team, the couple wouldn't be able to celebrate the company of one another each and every day.

Case Study – Senior with Difficult Personality Makes It Hard to Keep Aides

Client: Paul

Scenario:

Daughter Terry is the sole caretaker for her father, Paul. She worries she can't enlist help because he will be rude or inappropriate toward them.

Family and Support:

Paul has five children but is estranged from four. Terry cared for him until she enlisted our agency. Paul eventually reached out to his other children after our caregiver helped him reconnect with his emotions.

Considerations:

The biggest obstacle was Paul's willingness. He was adamant about letting only Terry assist, rejecting agency involvement. Terry was embarrassed to bring in caregivers because her father was sarcastic and rude toward them. It was difficult for him to have a female caretaker because he was especially inappropriate with women. He needed frequent medical visits because he had kidney failure, congestive heart failure, and fibrillation.

Judy: Early on in our business, we had a very sarcastic client, Paul. I had met his daughter, Terry, at a networking event.

When I told her about my profession, she said, "I need your help, but I'm embarrassed for you to meet my father. He's a very gruff, very difficult man. He's extremely sarcastic; he can be very inappropriate. I brought in another agency, and they said they couldn't provide care, he was so rude."

Terry and her husband were planning a trip for her 50th birthday, but she was concerned about leaving since her father wouldn't allow any other caretakers. At the time, he required two or three medical visits every week.

I said, "This will be a perfect open door. You deserve a trip for your birthday, and you're going to take your trip. We will start to provide care while you're away."

Terry told Paul I would be visiting. He was crass, sarcastic, and slightly inappropriate; even a little flirtatious. My own father had sarcastic tendencies, so it wasn't anything that I couldn't handle. Once he understood my intervention would alleviate his daughter's care responsibilities for a much-needed vacation, he finally agreed to let my agency assist.

He leaned forward, touched me and said, "Will you find me a beautiful woman?"

I said, "No, but I have a man in mind who might look good in a dress."

He burst out laughing and told his daughter he loved me, and that we were great friends. He was now on board. I assigned a male caregiver, Christian, to visit Paul for companionship and to escort him to medical appointments because he had several medical conditions that rendered him unstable.

On the third visit, his caregiver brought him lasagna, and Paul asked, "Why are you doing this?"

Christian replied, "Because I love you."

They became great friends and Paul looked forward to his time with his caregiver. When Terry came back from vacation, Paul wanted Christian to continue. This finally allowed Terry to go back to running her business.

Paul had five children, but he was estranged from the other four. Terry had told me her siblings stopped speaking to Paul because he'd been so difficult toward them during their lifetime. He had made some bad decisions, hurting their mother very much, thus hurting them. They no longer wanted anything to do with him.

Christian was wonderful and prayed with Paul.

The first time they prayed, Paul said, "Would you write that prayer down?"

Paul said the prayer every day after that. He eventually reached out to his other children and reconnected with them.

Then there was a Friday that Christian needed to take Paul to a doctor's visit, but when he showed up, no one came to the door. We called 911. Terry lived around the corner and beat the EMT to the house.

She couldn't muster the courage to go inside and pleaded with Christian, "Please go in. You need to go in; I can't go in without you."

Christian went in and found Paul had passed away the night before.

Terry said to us countless times - "I don't know what I would have done without you. In the six months you provided care, I was able to get my life back. I was able to run my business. I was able to do things with my husband and go out to dinner for the first time in years."

She credited Christian for showing her father how to love people again, allowing him to reconnect with his children and understand how to communicate that love. She also thanked him for being there when her father had passed away. She really needed that support. Our caregiver spoke at his funeral, and Paul's children felt so blessed that Christian had not only befriended their father but had also changed his life in the process.

Case Study – Sweet little woman in need of assistance and companionship; Husband suffered brain injury

Client: Gayle and Robert

Scenario:

The agency met Gayle when she was 88 and her husband, Robert, was 90. Their Elder Care Financial Planner was caring for them and reached out to our agency, but the couple and their daughter canceled because of financial concerns. Robert fell, suffered a head injury, and was signed into a nursing home. Gayle, now living alone, was at risk of falling and was experiencing delirium.

Family and Support:

Their only daughter, Denise, lived out-of-state and was not emotionally-equipped to support. Gayle's financial planner, Tim, had known Gayle for 40 years and was a very good adviser. Tim reached out to our agency.

Considerations:

Insecurity about finances, but not an *actual* financial hardship, prevented Gayle from engaging care agencies. The client was at risk for falls, and could not drive. Gayle's considerations: How do I stay safe where I live, and how do I visit my husband? It took time to build trust between the client and the caretakers. The clients suffered from delirium and needed reassurance.

Judy: Gayle and Robert's Elder Care Financial Planner, Tim, had known the couple for 40 years. We met him at an expo and he said he had a client he thought could use our help. Gayle and Robert needed housekeeping assistance once a week because the laundry room was in the basement and the trek was becoming too dangerous for the elderly couple.

Gayle and Robert were a really neat couple; very much in love. They built a nice, sweet little ranch house once Robert returned from World War II and had been living there for 65 years. They told stories of how in love they were, and how Gayle anxiously awaited his homecoming when he was away in the war. She would enjoy going to the dance hall with her future sister-in-law, Mary, waiting for the men to return.

After two visits, I believe their daughter, Denise, convinced her parents it was too expensive to have housekeeping, so they canceled our service after a short time. Tiny four-foot, ten-inch Gayle had already taken numerous falls, and Robert was her primary caregiver. About three months after they canceled service, Robert was heading to the basement to do laundry, fell down the stairs, and hit his head. He went straight to the hospital and into rehabilitation. He suffered a very severe brain injury and ultimately passed away in the skilled nursing facility. During this time, Denise had to move out of state, a few thousand miles away.

We were immediately re-engaged to provide service by the Elder Care Financial Planner, who called me and said, "It's not your fault, but services should never have been canceled. Now Robert is supposed to come home from rehab and Gayle cannot take care of him. We need care in place all day long."

Gayle was alone, and she already experienced 13 falls in one year. She typically fell while getting dressed in the morning and undressed in the evening. Many incidents had to do with dehydration and low blood pressure. We started visiting her daily, every morning and evening. We prepared her breakfast, helped her get dressed, and did housekeeping. It was companionship, really. We would play games and talk with her. She missed her husband very much, so we would bring her to visit him in the nursing home. She expressed how she wanted to die at home, not in a nursing home or hospital; that was her plea.

She had hesitations at first, but she came to love our caregivers. They laughed together, and she could cry to them. I have this image of her: She was getting ready to visit Robert in the hospital and she's leaning against her sink in her bathroom. This little 88-year-old woman, using a mirror to look at the back of her hair to make sure she looked beautiful enough. She matched her jewelry to her sweaters — pink earrings, pink sweater; green earrings, green sweater. Her shoes matched so perfectly.

She loved her Hallmark movies and Dancing with the Stars. She had beautiful plants, and the most beautiful Christmas cactus I've ever seen. She advised me on my planting. She had this great sense of humor and was an overall lovely lady.

Robert died about four months after he returned to the nursing home. I would drop by to check up on Gayle from time to time.

One evening she leaned over and she said to me, "You know, I might be crazy, but I talk to his picture sometimes."

I said, "You know when my husband passes I think I'll probably talk to his picture."

One night, before we were on 24-hour care, her daughter called me around 11:00 PM.

Denise said, "Judy, I called my mother about a half an hour ago and I didn't like the sound of her voice, so I called 911 and they took her by ambulance. What will I do if they don't admit her to the hospital? I'm far away."

I told her to have the emergency room call me.

Sure enough, at 2:00 a.m., the emergency room called me and they said, "We have a little lady here who says that you can be called any time of the night and you would come and get her."

"Yes, that's true."

So off I went to retrieve her, brought her back to her house, made sure she had some water, helped her in the bathroom, and put her safely to bed. Then I locked the door.

Our caregiver arrived the next morning.

This happened right after we recommended 24-hour care be put in place. Our caregivers were really good at navigating delirium and dementia and Gayle had some trouble with delirium, thinking neighbors were having loud parties all night long.

When the time came, we referred her to hospice care. She had a hospital bed placed in her bright, sunny living room where she had wanted it. During the last three days of Gayle's life, Denise came to the house but wanted our caregivers to stay. Denise wanted to sleep through the night, so our caregivers were with the family all day and all night. Gayle eventually passed away at home, which is just what she wanted.

Bio

Judy has always had a passion for stories, a favorite memory is at the public library with her mother. So, it is no surprise that what gives Judy the most pleasure now is to connect with the elderly and to hear their stories. It is her desire to know someone deeper that creates a sense of warmth and caring.

Judy started her career as a physical therapist after graduating from Northeastern University in 1985. With more than 25 years in the field of rehabilitation, Judy's career changed directions when her mother had a stroke. Feeling called to do more for those who desired to stay home as they aged, Judy opened her New Hampshire agency in 2012. With a passion for learning and giving, Judy is a Certified Senior Advisor and a Certified Dementia Practitioner. Judy teaches on a variety of topics related to senior care and is the host of the "Caring for Seniors" segment on a New Hampshire radio program, Girard at Large.

Probably due to years assisting children and adults with varying disabilities reach their highest level of independence, Judy continues to seek ways to help others maintain independence and dignity throughout the lifespan. The unique challenges of caring for those with dementia is a special calling for Judy and this is where the understanding of how our stories are used to create an improved quality of life blends with Judy's ability to listen, to collaborate, and to teach.

Faith is at the center of each day for Judy. Each client, family member, and caregiver is on Judy's heart and in her prayers. So often, as we age our need to understand the end of life includes a spiritual aspect, and the elderly connect on a deeper level with their faith. Judy's ability to offer support to aging clients and families, and to connect people, is a gift to those in need.

Both the young and the old teach us daily how to be present, attend to the moment, listen, hold a hand, watching for changes in expression and posture to find a common thread, a familiar story.

The joy of the shared life and a shared story is what Judy celebrates as the owner of a home health care agency franchise in New Hampshire.

Judy Loubier, PT, CSA, CDP

Owner/Executive Director

603-801-1936

Haytham Najjar

How long have you been in home health care, and how did you get into it?

Haytham: I've been in home health care since 1990. I was formerly in the hospitality industry, working in hotels and restaurants, which is what I studied in college. My goal was to own or a franchise a restaurant. Several years later, after having tried that, I found it wasn't my passion, so I decided to change careers entirely.

I didn't know home care at the time and took a position with an agency where I worked for about five years and grew with them as they opened multiple offices. I found a liking for this service and decided it was something I wanted to pursue myself. My final position with them was Branch Manager for a location that I opened, hired for, and ran.

My take away in this experience was what not to do, particularly, in terms of ethics and working with clients; I decided to combine my experience in hospitality and home care. and started my own agency.

When I started the business, I wanted to have a good, reputable agency that was going to provide outstanding service. And I think we've been successful after 22 years in business. We are well respected and part of the local community.

What's your professional background training?

Haytham: I earned my Bachelor of Science and Business degree with a focus in Hospitality Administration. While I had no prior professional training in nursing or home care; I do have a caring heart and hired a team of professionals who are the medical/nursing side of the business. What we as a team pride ourselves on is being proactive, to prevent and resolve an issue. We have a "Consider it done" approach when addressing the needs or concerns of our clients. I consistently rely on my hospitality training and experience to ensure we provide a solution rather than an excuse.

Home health care is a touching business. What's your passion, that gets you up day after day?

Haytham: I pride myself in providing an outstanding level of care and with each new day, I attempt to surpass it. I continually remind my staff that while we are proud of the work we do; the biggest room is room for improvement.

Tell me about your agency, CarePlus Home Health, and the types of clients you help.

Haytham: CarePlus is licensed by the Maryland Department of Health and Mental Hygiene as a level 3 residential service agency (RSA) We provide services that include skilled nursing, assistance with activities of daily living (ADLs) and non-skilled care (companions) for clients in their homes., Through our thorough intake process, our home care experts gather the information needed, our RNs assess and develop a plan of care for every client and appropriately place skilled, carefully screened professional caregivers to provide care that's specifically tailored to our clients' individual needs. We also provide education, training, and services for our caregivers and employees.

What geographic area is served?

Haytham: Our service area includes Maryland and Washington, DC with our highest concentration currently in Montgomery County, MD.

How many patients do you work with at a time?

Haytham: While our volume of clients fluctuates from week to week, we prepared to provide care to about 100 clients at any given time.

What are the most common obstacles that prevent your clients from being able to stay in their home and get the care they need?

Haytham: Only in a certain circumstance such as if a client is in need of acute care or skilled nursing care in rehab or family dynamics require a client to move.

What would your advice be to the reader who is serious about helping a loved one remain at home with care?

Haytham: I would recommend speaking to a Geriatric Care Manager or Aging Life Care Expert (aginglifecare.org), who is local in your community or contact the local Area Agency on Aging (www.n4a.org). These professionals specialize in the services and home care agencies available and can refer you the appropriate service.

Are there any pitfalls that the reader should be aware of? What should they look for in choosing someone to help them?

Haytham: The most important thing is to find a reputable, licensed agency. The pitfalls include hiring an unlicensed service or choosing to hire an individual who is not professionally vetted based on a referral from a friend. Reputable agencies will screen their caregivers, which at a minimum include: Verification of license/certification, criminal background check, professional and personal references, health screening, skill and competency assessments, and using the e-verify system for document authenticity.

Is there anything that patients and their families can do to prepare for working with you?

Haytham: Yes, it's most helpful when clients are knowledgeable of their family or friends' potential needs and can provide this information accurately during our initial intake.

It helps us for the caller to know what the potential goals are and the client's personal situation. for us to make recommendations on how to provide care and help keep the client at home. However, we do not try to sell our services to some people who may be inappropriate for home care.

Is there anything else you want to add?

Haytham: Yes. Because the cost of care is out-of-pocket, I am a proponent of long-term care insurance, which can help defray the cost or help pay for most of it.

Case Study - Married Couple with Round the Clock Care Needs

Client: Serge and Lucy

Scenario:

Married couple Serge and Lucy have moved to assisted living as Lucy has trouble walking, and has dementia and needs round the clock care. Serge felt the facility was not taking good care of Lucy and wanted to move. After a few unsuccessful moves, followed by Serge falling and needing care himself, they moved back to senior apartments bringing in 24-hour care to provide satisfactorily for both their needs.

Family and Support:

The couple moved a few states away to be near their children, who were supportive, but not available as caregivers due to busy work schedules.

Considerations:

While Serge was unhappy with the level of care at the assisted living facility, after his wife's health declined, and he needed help after a fall, he realized that they needed round the clock care. He opted to move into senior apartments and manage the level of care and his choice of providers via our home care agency.

Haytham: Serge and Lucy Fontana knew each other from the town where they grew up. They began dating in 1943. When Lucy was in high school, Serge joined the Navy, where he spent three years. After he was discharged, he went to a Midwestern university to continue his education. Lucy would come out to see Serge for dances and events and Serge would book a hotel room for her when she visited. They got married in 1950 after Serge graduated from the university. He then joined the "bureau" (FBI) where he had 500 people working under him.

His job required traveling and they had their first child while living in the South. They moved to the West Coast, where child number 2 was born, but he was sent back home to the East Coast because the Italian mafia was becoming predominant, and since Serge was Italian, he was assigned to work there. They moved into the New York area where they lived for 30 years and finally moved to the Washington D.C. area to be closer to their adult children.

As they grew older, Lucy and Serge were both suffering from back pain. He had a back operation, which was successful, and he suggested she do the same. Unfortunately, her operation did not go as well, and she could no longer walk without a walker due to the operation.

They had 3 children: two girls and a boy, but they lost their first-born child to cancer at the age of 50. Lucy developed dementia in 2012. Their daughters settled in the Washington D.C. metro area in 2014, from the New York area, where Lucy and Serge were living. He had put a stair lift in their house for Lucy, but as her condition became worse, both mentally & physically, they decided to move to Maryland to be closer to their children.

They moved into Senior Apartments for a couple years, where Lucy fell twice within six months of each other. In each fall, she broke the same femur and had to have two operations, which limited her mobility even more. Serge became her primary caregiver and he would care for her at night until he couldn't do it anymore.

They moved into an assisted living community, but Serge felt that Lucy wasn't being treated well so they tried another assisted living, but they weren't satisfied there either. Serge moved Lucy into a skilled nursing facility at a continuing care retirement community and because he was very close to her and could interpret her feelings, he would stay with her 12-hours a day at the nursing home. The staff must have thought "I was a pain in the ass" because he was there every day from 10 am until 10 pm. Sometimes she would cry, and he would talk to her and calm her down.

Serge was getting ready to also move into the same retirement community, and then he fell outside and couldn't get up. He had to call his daughter for help. They decided to move back to the senior apartments and signed up with CarePlus Home Health to receive 24-hour care with their aide Unice, whom they've grown to love. Serge says Lucy has improved tremendously; she can speak much better than she used to, and Lucy and Unice had an immediate connection, even though Lucy was afraid of people in her home.

Serge said "CarePlus guiding us to the right doctor was great. He was the right fit for Lucy. He tweaked her medicine, so she can sleep throughout the night. I think it's safe to say I love you as much as you love me."

"CarePlus has literally been a plus to me in that I can depend on you. I'm not asking for anything special although you treat me very special, because all this time, I was taking care of her and things, I had 2 heart operations; now I don't have to carry the burden of being her caregiver."

Case Study – Single Man Injured on the Job

Client: Griffin

Scenario:

After being injured on the job, Griffin moved from rehab to an assisted living facility, where we began providing care. He later moved into his home and has been receiving live-in care since.

Family and Support:

Griffin lives alone. His sister lives nearby.

Considerations:

A major element of home care and especially a 24/7 live-in arrangement is both finding the most appropriate caregiver and matching client and caregiver personalities. When the client is in an assisted living community, their caregiver must follow the community's rules and the lines aren't always clear as to who's responsible for what as the resident is receiving care from both the community and the home care agency. Lastly, receiving payment through an insurance company is often challenging.

Haytham: Griffin was referred to us by an insurance broker. When we became involved, Griffin was already in assisted living recovering from a hospitalization followed by a rehab stay. He had been injured on the job, and as such, his care was to be paid for by his former employer's workers compensation carrier.

Initially, we provided private duty home care while Griffin was in an assisted living community. While he was receiving assistance, he still needed additional one-on-one care because they could only provide care for short increments of 30 minutes at a time. Certain residents who need extra care are sometimes asked to hire their additional outside help. We became involved and provided one-on-one, private duty care within the assisted living community.

Once his condition improved enough, he moved back home. Griffin has a sister close by but lives alone. We're continuing live-in care and assist with scheduling appointments, preparing his daily meals. It's going well.

When you have someone living with you 24/7, personality compatibility comes into play. You don't want somebody who talks too much, and you also don't want someone who doesn't engage enough; it has to be the right fit. So, matching becomes a big part of that process.

Another challenge is finding live-in caregivers who can also drive when the patient is in need of transportation. It's even more of a challenge in our specific area because live-in caregivers must also be CNA certified. Most agencies aren't able to provide a live-in caregiver, let alone one who also drives. Griffin is still a client of ours and is happy with his live-in caregiver. Meanwhile, we are happy to continue providing care, we visit him regularly, and keep in touch with his sister.

Case Study– Elderly Couple in Need of Care and Financially Supporting Disabled Son

Client: Rob and Sue Cohen

Scenario:

A couple in their 90s living at home in need of around-the-clock care.

Family and Support:

The Cohens lived in Bethesda, Maryland and had a disabled adult son Mark, who lives in Washington, DC. Their other son, Elliot, lives in New England and set up the initial care consultation by phone. The elderly couple is, in turn, providing financial support for Mark. No other family lives locally.

Considerations:

It is often necessary for agencies to make decisions on behalf of a client, but they must recognize their limitations when advocating. The client's safety and care must be the primary concern in decision-making. Adverse weather conditions can pose dangers to the elderly and obstacles in the transportation of caregivers to clients. This story poses a slightly different situation than the others, as I was personally involved.

Haytham: The clients' names were Rob and Sue Cohen. They lived in Bethesda, Maryland. Their son, Elliot, was referred to us through our website. He called us, set up service, and we began to care for his parents. Initially for Mrs. Cohen for whom we secured a live-in because the couple was in their 90s and needed supervision throughout the day and night. Rob and Sue lived in a home that was prone to multiple power losses at either extreme; in the summertime heat, or wintery cold. They were a frail, elderly couple and wheelchair bound. When power losses overtook the home, I would ensure they could stay somewhere safe. With Elliot's permission, I would personally transport them to an accessible hotel room to safely stay for a night or two, along with their caregivers, and I would bring them back home after ensuring their power was restored. We provided that extra level of care for them and many of our clients.

We cared for them for nearly nine years, which is quite a long time in the home care industry. About five years into our service, we recognized they needed a dedicated care manager, who could oversee their daily medical needs beyond what we could provide as a home care agency. This included making sure multiple doctor's appointments were scheduled and managed, groceries and supplies were ordered, and keeping in regular communication with their son, Elliot since there was no local family support. We identified and referred them to an appropriate *geriatric care manager*, who was also a nurse. The care manager would visit weekly, working in conjunction with our agency to ensure the best care for this family.

Eventually, Mr. & Mrs. Cohen's needs called for additional around-the-clock care, as both patients conditions declined, requiring them to have 36 hours of care each day, or a live-in caregiver plus two 12-hour shifts per day. This continued until Mr. Cohen passed away, then we continued with a live-in caregiver for Mrs. Cohen until her family finally decided to move her to Colorado, where they had recently relocated to. We received notice that she passed on a couple of years ago.

This story shows how heartwarming and very touching experiences like this can be. You can't help but develop a strong relationship and become attached to your clients while ensuring they receive our service. My team performs little miracles like this every day and we ensure our clients always have the best care in place. I also make myself available to our caregivers during snowstorms to drive them to their jobs when they're snowbound and ensure they have work and our clients have coverage.

Finally, as a way to give back to my community, I am on the board and current president of our local networking organization called GROWS, the Grass Roots Organization for the Well-being of Seniors, which also advocates for seniors, provides education, and community outreach since 1989. I'm very excited and energized to help make the eldercare care community a better place in Montgomery County, Maryland.

Bio

Haytham [Tom] Najjar is the founder and owner of CarePlus Home Health, Inc. Haytham graduated from Florida State University with a business degree in Hospitality Administration; he spent several years working in hotels and managing various restaurants in the Washington DC metro area.

Using his hospitality experience, he embarked on a new career in the eldercare community. Haytham saw the need for affordable, quality services that considered each client's unique needs and personalizing the care provided. As a result, in 1995 he launched CarePlus Home Health with a mission to provided professional, compassionate care to individuals while maintaining their independence and quality of life. Haytham's vision is for CarePlus to be a partner, advocate, and friend to our clients and their families during a challenging and transitional period in their loved one's lives. Haytham had the opportunity to personally utilize his staff when his own father needed care in the last months of his life in 2000.

CarePlus Home Health, Inc.

http://www.CarePlusInc.com

301-740-8870

Tom@careplusinc.com

Nicole Peretti

Note: Nicole's role in the home health care industry is different from the other authors in this book.

Could you tell me about your role in home health care? How long have you been in this role, and how did you get into it?

Nicole: Sure. I don't own a home care company, and I don't think I ever will own a home care company, but I work very closely with many people who do.

I got into the industry because of my relationship with Steve. At this point, we've known each other for 17 or 18 years, having met when we worked at the same company in college. After seeing what he was doing when he was running his home care business, I knew I didn't want to do that. But when he started this company, Hurricane Marketing Enterprises, I thought, "Oh, I can definitely do that! I can help people with sales and marketing; I can help people as a business coach; I can help people with the everyday struggles of running their business." That's how I got into working with Steve again. I learned a lot about the home health care industry from him, from other coaches, and from our clients. From that, we have now expanded to a nonprofit, The Institute for Dignity and Grace, which Steve and I co-founded last year.

That's where my experience in home health care comes in: I help our clients who are running their own home care companies. I take it to the next level through Dignity and Grace with raising funds and awareness, as well as lobbying in Washington, where we fight for funding for the home care industry and for our seniors. I have never had any home care clients myself, but I have family members who have used home care services. I have seen firsthand how life-changing it can be for the seniors and also for their families. I feel as though by reaching out through many different organizations, talking to all our clients — my clients specifically — and the people with the nonprofit, I'm taking care of millions of home care clients.

What is your professional background and training?

Nicole: I worked in marketing roles for a couple of different companies. I went to college for marketing; but of course, when you're 18 and you're in college, you don't really know what you want to do with your life. I got put into this business track, and I said, "I want to do business-something, but

I don't know what, exactly." I started learning more about marketing as I went through college, and I realized that I liked it. So, it worked out that I ended up majoring in marketing in college.

I had a lot of retail jobs when I was in high school and college, and I liked selling and interacting with people. I got excited about the thrill of making a sale. Then, I was in more of a management role, teaching people how to make sales on their own. That's what ignited my work right now: a lot of sales background.

Steve and I met at a job that we had when we were both in college. We didn't go to school together, but we met while in college, selling Cutco knives for Vector Marketing. We learned a lot at that company that we've put into play here in this business. The strategies and techniques are very similar for marketing any high-end item, be it knives or home care. In the end, my background in sales, management training, and organizational leadership helps me in this role here.

So, I have a marketing background, a sales background, and an H.R. background; and I do a lot of that here. I help our clients with all those things as well. Home health care is an incredible industry, and I love what I do.

What's your passion? What keeps you going, day after day?

Nicole: That's a really good question. Aging is something that affects everybody at one time or another in their life: you see someone you care about getting sick and older and struggling with day-to-day tasks, and it impacts your own life as well. I was going through that scenario myself, with my grandparents. Through working in this industry with these clients and our nonprofit, I'm finding that it's a sensitive subject. It's very tough for people to be in it daily.

For me, it's about helping people. It's making them feel that there is somebody who cares and is their companion. It's huge for a lot of people: maybe they don't live with anybody, or maybe they do, but that person has other responsibilities and things that they need to do. Having a companion to be there with them, just to look through old photo albums and stuff; that's sometimes life-changing.

How can we make this person's life better? How can we make them feel of value… for seniors specifically? They have so much to offer, and I think they are forgotten, especially in this culture. It's always rush, rush, rush, and work, work, work; my kids and my job and my husband. You forget about your parents or your grandparents, or even about the old lady that lives next door; the life that they've had, and the experience that they can share. It's fascinating to talk with them. We should honor and respect our elders. That's what we're taught as children; but then when we grow up and become adults, so many of us forget to do that.

For me personally, it's become a passion. I didn't know I had that passion until I started working in this industry. Being around the seniors — really respecting them, taking care of them, seeing their value, and nurturing them — you start to think, "Hey, let's look at your photo albums. Tell me a story about your life." I learned a lesson from that. I think that's awesome. That's what gets me going. I think, "What else can I learn?" You learn best from other people's life experiences, I believe.

Tell me about your work in marketing and the type of clients you help

Nicole: With this business, we specifically work in what's known as the Private Duty Home Care Industry. Traditionally, these are owners of businesses that serve the elderly. They could have other clients as well, but mainly it's seniors. This is something that seniors or their family members typically must pay for out of pocket, so it's a difficult industry to be in. There are lots of people who need the service but don't know that it exists, what it entails, how to find it, or how to make it work in their schedule. The clients that we're working with are dealing with that on a day to day basis: they're constantly explaining their services and how they can help people.

Their organizations hire caregivers who are assigned to certain patients, and the caregivers go to the house and take care of the patient. It may be something as simple as making breakfast, taking the trash out, and then watching television or playing cards together. Or, it may be something a little bit more serious or more healthcare-related — helping them walk into the bathroom to take a shower, or helping them use the bathroom and cleaning them up — all while preventing potential injuries within the home and keeping them safe.

Our clients are business owners who are dealing with the fact that this is a very difficult industry to be in. For most other businesses, of course, there are ups and downs. You lose clients and you gain clients, and that's normal. But in this industry, when you lose a client, it's sometimes — or more often — because the client has died. I think that's a very difficult thing that not a lot of people rarely pay attention to or realize. These business owners are losing business, but they're also losing a person whom they've potentially met many times over many years, about whom they cared... and now this person is gone. I find that some of the greatest people, with the biggest hearts, are these home care company owners. They give and give and give. I feel so blessed to be in this industry, working with them and helping them.

What are the most common obstacles you hear from your clients that prevent their patients from being able to stay in their homes and get the care they need?

Nicole: Some of the most common obstacles that I hear about are issues with the family. For instance, maybe one child lives out of state and another child lives nearby, and they argue over who should take care of what, who should pay for what, and who should handle the situation. They *know* mom needs help, but who's going to take care of it? So, you bring in a third party: a home care company. Now you have a stranger in the mix, essentially, who are trying to direct what everyone should do. And the siblings argue over that too. This is very common. It's normal that everybody has a common goal of wanting to help their parents — their loved ones — in this difficult situation, but it's hard to get everybody on the same page. That's one common obstacle.

Another obstacle involves the seniors themselves. Oftentimes, when people in their 70s, 80s, and 90s are struggling, it's a huge change from when they were in their 20s or so when they were growing up very independently. They've lived through tough times. People who are seniors now grew up very, very differently than we do now. At 20 they were probably married, owned a house, and had been working for a couple of years — very independent adults at that point. But now, many 20-year-olds are still living with mom and dad and have no idea how to do anything. When a senior who has done everything themselves for the past 50 or 60 years, and suddenly needs help *now*, it's very difficult for them to accept that. They're resistant to it, and understandably so. I think they want to feel like, "I'm still in charge. I'm still your dad. I can do it myself. I don't need help." It's hard for them to admit that they do. That's a big struggle, not only for the home care company but also for the family members; because they see their dad is changing. His role is changing, and he's sad and angry and scared. All these emotions are normal, and I see them frequently.

But each individual person thinks that they're going through it on their own. It's important to make sure everybody knows this is normal: this period of time, this indecision, this craziness of figuring out how we are going to take care of the last part of your life. This is not what people plan for. When you think about planning out your life, you plan on getting married, buying your first house, having kids, growing up and getting your job, having vacations… you plan all the good stuff, but you don't really plan the bad stuff until it happens.

Everybody goes through this, and it's completely normal. If we can talk about it, and if the patients and their families can understand that the home care owners have seen this a lot, they will realize that the owners know what they're talking about and are experts in this situation. As a patient, or as a family member of a patient who needs the services, you put your trust into a person who has seen this many times before. They really do have your best interests at heart. They're here to take care of you.

What would your advice be to the reader who is serious about helping a loved one remain at home?

Nicole: I think communication is important. Talk to them about what they want specifically; keep them involved in the conversation and decision-making process. Unless there are medical reasons why they really can't be involved, keep them in it as long as they can and as much as they can. That way, they don't feel that it's being put upon them; they're not being told, "This is what you're doing. This is what's happening." They're making decisions, such as, "I like this company" or "I like this person" or "I want these hours for my care." It helps them with the decision-making process, and it also helps them accept that this is what they need. It's going to keep them safe, ultimately.

Second, readers should make sure that they are doing their research. You have a lot of different options out there in terms of types of care, levels of care, and maybe whether or not to put them into a facility. Certainly, keeping someone at home and keeping them safe is important, as is listening to an expert. It's important to go by the advice of the social workers and people who know what they're talking about. You might say, "Well, I only need someone to help her get out of bed in the morning and make sure she had breakfast, and then I need someone to come over at night and make sure she had dinner and goes to bed." You think that's sufficient because those are the two difficult things that mom needs help with. But what about the middle of the day? Is she going to sit in a chair all day and do nothing and be alone? That's not really the best care.

I think about it as a holistic situation. What services could be provided throughout the day, and what benefits would come from that? It's important to do your research, pay attention to specific needs, and communicate with everybody involved.

Are there any pitfalls that the reader should be aware of? What should they look for in choosing someone to help their loved one?

Nicole: This is a tough one. There are several common issues.

My first advice when you're looking for a home care company is to go with someone who is licensed, bonded, and insured. That is number one. It's very easy to look through Craigslist, or ask a friend of a friend who says, "My sister can take care of your grandma." Sure. But then what happens if grandma falls while this person is taking care of her? A lot of things can go wrong when you're taking care of someone who's elderly and potentially sick, injured, or recovering from an injury. You want to make sure you have someone who's fully trained.

You also need a company, a home care agency, because they have multiple caregivers. Caregivers are people too, and things come up. This is their job, and they may have to call out occasionally. Maybe they get sick, or their child gets sick, or some emergency comes up and they can't make it to work. If you're working with a home care company, they can send someone in place of that caregiver; whereas if you're working with the lady who lives up the road, if she can't come then nobody comes, and then your loved one is left alone. So, I always recommend finding a company that is reputable and has all their bases covered, with multiple caregivers and a system for call outs.

The agencies have licensing, insurance, and bonding, and all their caregivers go through background checks. They're doing all the essential things to make sure they're putting a qualified caregiver in your home. If anything goes wrong, they're going to take care of it for you because they're a business; they're providing a service and they're backing it up with those extra little things behind the scenes that you don't really think about until you need them.

What's the biggest misconception about home health care?

Nicole: I think the biggest misconception is what home health care providers do, specifically. It's kind of seen as a babysitting service; as if I'm simply watching grandma, but not really taking care of the whole situation. Clients are missing the multiple levels of what they're doing as a home care provider: providing services focused on one person, being a companion, keeping the client safe, keeping them happy, and giving them a better quality of life.

Think about your older loved ones and what they've gone through their whole life. Now they're at the end, whether they die in a year or they die in five or ten years. At this point, they're in that last stage of their life, and you want to make it comfortable for them. You hope that they're able to still have the things that they love: participating in the same hobbies and interests if possible or even having their favorite foods. It can simple; maybe they really get a lot of joy out of having a cup of tea every morning with some cookies. The caregiver can provide that, whereas if they were alone, maybe they couldn't do it on their own.

Being a caregiver is a lot of work. It's sometimes not recognized or appreciated, but it should be valued and rewarded. I think that it's an essential function nowadays, especially with our society as it is: everyone's busy and working; people have jobs and kids and soccer games, and more to go to and do. Then you have to take care of mom or dad, or both, and having a caregiver there who does more than just wipe their butts really helps. Sometimes I need someone who can not only make sure she uses the toilet properly and make sure she takes a shower, but someone who can bond with her, be her friend, and take care of her; keep her comfortable and give her the best time at the end of her life. With the nonprofit, we talk about aging in place with dignity and grace. That's what good home care does for seniors.

That's really where this caregiving comes in. If your mom likes gardening, then the caregiver can take her outside and plant a flower; or maybe she would enjoy baking cookies, or reading, or playing cards. It enables them to continue to do those things with another person who's there strictly for them. The caregiver is 100 percent devoted to your loved one; taking care of that person is all they do. One might think, "Oh I want them to clean the house," okay; but they're also there to take care of grandma. So, I think that's the biggest misconception: what a caregiver's job responsibilities are.

Is there anything that patients and their families can do to prepare for working with the home care company?

Nicole: Yes. For one, know exactly what kind, and what level of care you would need. Maybe that comes from a doctor, or nurse, or a social worker, but know what you're looking for specifically. Maybe grandma tends to get up in the middle of the night and wander around, and everyone in the house is sleeping except for her, so you might need somebody who's live-in or comes in at night specifically.

Another thing would be, obviously, to know the plan of care, including medications and anything else health-related. If there's dialysis if they might need to go to physical therapy or speech therapy… the company needs to be aware of those things before assigning a caregiver, and before starting services, so that they can find the best caregivers most qualified to work with your loved one. That's very important.

Again, do your research. If your loved one is in the hospital or in rehab, and they're being discharged and sent home, and a social worker or a nurse recommends that you need home care, they may suggest a company they work with, you should talk to them immediately. I would say sooner rather than later, absolutely. You plan for that discharge because you want to have something in place right away for when mom comes home; not, "Oh well, I'm bringing her home and then I'll call the home care company and see what we can do." You want her to be safe and have a smooth transition immediately.

When you're researching home care companies, it's okay to have two or three options that you talk with before making a decision, because you want someone with whom you feel comfortable. Your mom or dad, or whoever needs the care, should meet with them as well. They should be involved in this process and give their okay on it. "You have to get one home care company, Mom. You have to go with somebody, but I'll let you pick who you want;" I think that's a fair way of doing it, and it helps with the decision-making process.

Anything else you want to add?

Nicole: In general, as I said before, it is a very challenging time. You're seeing changes in your family members and that puts a mirror on yourself. Suddenly, you're in a new role, to parent the parent. For most people, it's really difficult.

It's important to realize that there are many companies out there that specialize in helping seniors. Most of the people — I don't want to say all — but most of the people who work for those companies genuinely care about seniors, and are passionate about what they're doing. Yes, they're going to make some money out of it; but the important thing is they care almost as much as you do about the health, safety, and comfort of your loved ones. They're very passionate about it. So, trust them and listen to their advice, and take what they say to heart. Always know that you're not alone in this process. This is normal; everyone's going through it.

So it's okay. We — the home care companies, home care providers, caregivers, owners, nurses, marketers, everybody involved — are here to help you help your loved one with this transition, and to make it smooth and keep them safe. That's why we're doing that. we feel your heart. We really do.

I get really into it now. It was already an inspiring cause, and it's such a crazy coincidence that my mom needed some help for my grandparents after we started the project. I totally relate to what the reader is going through because I have gone through it myself, with my own family.

That's why I think that this book is so important. I don't think any book like this exists specifically for finding home care. Nowadays, with the baby boomers, this generation needs to have some guidance, to know that they're not alone. I talk to people every day about senior care, and sometimes when we're talking, I'm crying because I can completely hear the struggles that they're dealing with: "I just want mom to be safe, I want this to go well, I need to be better, and maybe I can't do it myself anymore." That's hard for everyone, for sure.

Case Study – How home care helped three generations in one family find peace

The following is a personal recounting of my own Grandparents' experience with home care in addition to the impact their illnesses had on my parents as primary caregivers.

Scenario:

My Grandfather, Anthony Cavanna, was a 99-year-old who remained sharp in mind, but fragile in body. He needed some assistance and a reliable person to keep him from trying to do too much in a weakened state. My Grandmother, Violet, was physically strong and able but had Alzheimer's. My parents were under the constant pressure of providing appropriate care.

Family and Support:

Both my grandparents lived with my parents who could provide some care but weren't able to be full-time caregivers. There was also support from two sons, as well as local grandchildren.

Considerations:

The biggest concern was providing support on an as-needed basis and keeping my grandfather safe in the process. With such a sharp mind, he was always looking to do things beyond what he was capable of. My grandmother needed support for her physical and emotional needs and to be kept safe because she wasn't always aware of what was going on.

Nicole: This is a personal story told from the perspective of a *client* of a home care company, highlighting the effects it has not only on the couple in need but their adult children, as well.

My maternal grandparents moved into my parent's house when it became clear they could no longer function without assistance. They were both ill with their health declining rapidly, and we, unfortunately, thought they weren't going to be around much longer. My parents did *not* want to put them in a home, so the entire family decided it was safest to have them move in with my mom and dad. My dad was just about retired at the time and my mom owned a little clothing store on the side.

Due to the less stressful life of living with my parents, my grandparents started to get better and eventually thrive — they didn't have the stress of doing day-to-day maintenance on a house. My grandfather could now relax a little bit, and focus on living and spending time with my grandmother. He would give my dad a hard time for who-knows-what, just because, "He's the son in law, so I'm going to yell at him." But it made him healthy; it made him come back.

The same rejuvenation happened with my grandmother. I think most of her stress went away when she didn't have to worry about cleaning the house, grocery shopping, cooking, or laundry because now that was all taken care of. She still did those things when she wanted to, but not because she had to. Their quality of life was much more relaxed.

It was a very big decision to have my grandparents move in, and I was not expecting it to still be going on nearly 12 years later. At the time they moved into the house, my sister was still living there while she finished up college. So now all of a sudden, there were multiple generations living in the home, and renovations to the house had to be made. We had to modify who was sleeping in which bedroom and convert my dad's office into a sitting room for grandma and grandpa to watch tv and play cards. I think my grandparents felt like they were putting us out. It was an adjustment for everyone, no doubt, but for probably close to 10 years, everybody was happy and healthy, but then suddenly, the decline began. It started with my grandfather.

About seven or eight years into this arrangement, the dynamic started to change. Stress set in because my parents were now much older and retired and wanted to enjoy their life the way they envisioned it. It was around this time the health status of my grandparents began to decline. My parents couldn't travel like they wanted, and eventually, they couldn't even go out for a few hours without worrying about my grandparents falling and injuring themselves. They became trapped. They wanted to provide care and spend the time with them, but now care was absolutely necessary, and that put a lot of strain on the relationship between my parents and grandparents. This was a great concern to my sister and me, as we were seeing our own aging parents plagued by worry and stress.

I'm sure that my dad, at some point, thought "These aren't even my parents." He cared for them greatly, and beyond what many others in his shoes could do, but it was on a different level than my mom. It was harder on him, so there were times when he had to pull back from the situation. He certainly supported my mother, but he also wanted to live his life. My dad was 68, and he wanted to go out with my mom, and travel; he wanted to volunteer in the community and at the VA hospital; he wanted to do things he enjoys, but the situation prevented the freedom to do so. My parents had to cancel 2 or 3 vacations over the years because of the care needed back home. I think that my parents are incredibly strong for supporting each other through this process despite the strain on their marriage.

Taking on this role of caretaker for aging parents definitely changes the relationship between parent and a child. When the child becomes the caretaker, there's resentment and guilt, on both sides. It's important for the readers to know these feelings are totally normal. It feels terrible and it's very difficult to experience, but as I told my mom all the time, my clients tell me this is a normal occurrence, and she is not alone. If my mom wanted to have lunch with her friends, she felt obligated to either bring her mother or cancel the plans. There's a guilty feeling: "I have to tell my friend 'no,' and I don't want to do that, but I can't leave my mom. How could I possibly feel this way? She's my mom; of course, I need to take care of her as she took care of me. Why am I complaining about this?" It's a cycle of stress adult children of aging parents experience all the time.

My grandfather was a World War II combat medic; a hardcore, independent, tough guy. At the time we got home care, he had just turned ninety-nine and his mind was sharp, but his body was failing. It would take him 20 minutes to walk from one side of the house to the other. For me, it was so sad to see him in that internal struggle. Violet, my grandmother, had Alzheimer's but still had full use of her body — she could sweep the deck, go up and down the stairs — but she would lose track of what was happening. There were spurts when she was fairly lucid for months at a time, and others when she relapsed.

My grandparents were hopelessly devoted to each other. My grandfather always said that his purpose in life was to take care of my grandmother, and he was put on earth to do so. They had a great life together...raised three children, had six grandchildren, and 14 great-grandchildren. They would sit on the couch and hold hands. It was an incredibly loving and devoted relationship between the two of them.

For my grandfather to see his wife not recognize him sometimes, or not remember very important memories from their past, was devastating. She barely knew what day it was, but she was always up in the morning, picking out her outfits and accessorizing. She would put curlers in her hair every day. She swept the kitchen and fed the dog. She would tell the family stories about "her three husbands" all named Anthony (my grandfather). She would tell my grandfather her favorite husband was her first husband because he took her out on dates, then there was one who had kids with her, and lastly, her old man husband. Grandpa would listen, nod his head, and hold her hand.

Four years ago, around Thanksgiving, my grandfather had a few minor strokes, and they required him to stay in the hospital for a while. When he was released, we knew extra care was necessary to prevent him from trying to do too much on his own. As I said, he was very independent, so my parents hired a caregiver to keep him safe and help him with daily routines. It was a challenge getting my mom to realize that she couldn't do it on her own anymore, but once she gave in, the relief was instant.

Unfortunately, the caregiver was not present at the time of his fall in January. It was an early morning and he fell in the bathroom, hitting his head on the way down. He was severely hurt and almost bled out completely before he was discovered. His body temperature was down in the 70's at the hospital. He was fortunate to make a full recovery. Apparently, he was not ready to go; the "ultimate tough guy," he could do anything. He wanted to sit at the kitchen table every day, reading his newspaper and drinking his coffee like a grown man, so we needed the caregiver to assist him from walking from his hospital bed to the kitchen.

Both my parents were available to help, but my dad and mom wanted to make sure there would be somebody there during the times they were out of the house. We had a caregiver come in five days a week, so my parents could run errands and socialize. My dad volunteered, and my mom got to have lunch with her friends or visit my sister at our homes.

My grandfather was very, very independent. For example, if my dad asked him "Please don't do that. Please don't climb over the bar of the hospital bed, let us help you," he would yell at my dad, "No, don't tell me what to do!" But when the caregiver would ask, "Please Anthony, please don't climb over the bar, let me help you," he would listen because she was the caregiver. To him, the caregiver was a medical professional; not his son-in-law. Having been a medic in the war, I think the uniform — the scrubs — signified she was someone who knew what she was doing. She was there to help him, she had a job to do, and he respected that. He would be very defiant with my mom, very defiant with my dad, and kind of defiant with me and my sister, but whenever the *caregiver* told him to do something, he did it right away. So, the uniform was very important.

She made him feel like he wasn't being "taken care of," she was his teammate, in a lot of ways. Instead of her bringing him things, the caregiver took him to the things that he wanted to do. That's not always easy — he walked really slowly — but she hung with him the whole way, from the bedroom to the kitchen and back again. This made his final months better than they would have been. During that time with the caregiver, there was a huge improvement in his quality of life and my parents' quality of life.

This ultimately helped my sister and I feel better too, knowing our grandparents were receiving the proper care, and our parents were more relaxed and enjoying their retirement together. She provided support for all of us, even though she was there to take care of just grandpa. It's a trickledown effect

When my grandfather died, it was one month shy of his 100th birthday. My grandmother was holding his hand. They were soulmates. They had been very happily married over 70 years when he passed.

My family had discontinued home care after my grandfather passed for about a year and a half before my grandmother began to decline further. My family brought in another caregiver at this point, for what we call respite care; the client doesn't necessarily have medical needs, but it gives the primary caregiver a break.

We had one caregiver come on the weekends, and a different caregiver came two other weekdays. My grandmother took her caregivers on a trip down memory lane every single time they visited. She didn't remember showing them a photo album multiple times already; it was always a new thing in her mind. She told them the story of the love of her life, about her husband and children and her family growing up. They knew it well and I bet I could give the caregivers a family tree test and they would pass with flying colors.

The caregivers kept her company. They made sure she was eating healthy foods; otherwise she would eat a whole box of chocolates for lunch if you let her. They were with her when she was on the go, making sure she wasn't getting herself into any mischief or in danger of falling.

The caregiver gave my parents part of their freedom back again. My sister is a new mom, so my parents wanted to spend time with the baby and enjoy this newest stage of their life. Having someone at the house caring for my grandmother gave my parents the ability to do this.

When the caregiver was not there, I could see how difficult the struggle was for my parents. I would go to their house, stay for a weekend and become the caretaker for a couple of days. After only two days, I'd be stressed out. I can't even imagine what they went through, day in and day out, dealing with the care struggles of someone with Alzheimer's. Sometimes my grandmother would be mean for no obvious reason; sometimes she was very sad and inconsolable, and you can't reason with her and you ultimately don't know how to fix her problem. There would be times where my grandmother said very rude things to my mom, and we all wondered why. It wasn't her, it was the illness. You can rationalize that it's the illness until your face turns blue, but it still hurts in the moment, and it's hard to accept those constant comments from your own mother. This made my mom very sad, and it made her question herself.

My grandmother often got up in the middle of the night and got into mischief. Sometimes she would leave the house, and no one knew where she went. They would find her several doors down in cold weather. We would find her feeding the dogs in the middle of the night, dumping scoop after scoop into their bowls. She would wake up hungry, but didn't understand she had to cook the food; so she would eat the food right from the freezer. Once my mom woke up and realized, "Oh my god, she ate a frozen burrito. She just ate it frozen." This kind of situation creates guilt, stress and strain as a caregiver, and as a child who loves your parent in need.

This is definitely a story that needs to be told, a story a lot of people can relate to. My mom told me, "Just don't tell people that I stick my tongue out at your grandmother sometimes." And I said, "Yeah, but it's behind her back, and it's OK." But again, I stress to the reader, this is how you need to cope sometimes, and it's normal to feel this way. It's like taking care of a giant toddler in many ways, but they aren't learning and growing in a positive way like a child, they are getting worse and worse with each passing day. You know they aren't going to get better, and the only way it will stop is when they pass, and then all the guilty feelings come flooding in again. So, you make the decision to get home care, and you stick with that plan, get some peace of mind, and cope with this difficult situation any way you can.

My grandmother was still showering herself the last few months of her life. She put on her perfume, did her hair, and dressed herself. She passed in June of 2017, just shy of 97 years old.

Bio

Nicole Peretti is Director of Operations at *Hurricane Marketing Enterprises*, and co-founder of the nonprofit, The Institute for Dignity and Grace. Nicole graduated from Rowan University with a degree in Business Administration, with a specialization in Marketing. She oversees all the day-to-day operations of both businesses, ensuring they are run properly. Nicole is also a business coach and has worked one-on-one with many clients, who are typically home care business owners, from all over the country. She works closely with them to ensure they are using best practices and operating their companies with integrity and a focus on proper patient care.

Nicole lives in New Jersey with her two cats and enjoys drinking her morning coffee outside in her beautiful backyard. She loves reading, watching crime dramas on TV, spending time with family, and taking naps on weekends. While still in college, she started her sales career with *Cutco Cutlery*. Nicole has since managed sales teams for companies in several industries, but her favorite job is what she is doing now. Her passion and talent are in managing people, and that transfers into the work she does with her clients, teaching them how they can best interact with the people they meet and work with daily. She has personal experience with home care for her own family, as well as years of shared knowledge through her clients. Nicole truly cares about helping others, and that shows in all she does.

Institute for Dignity and Grace

848-863-6603

nicole@dignityandgrace.info

Resources

For additional information and resources please visit

http://dignityandgrace.info/resources/

90122058R00096

Made in the USA
Columbia, SC
01 March 2018